CATHOLIC VIEWER'S GUIDE

CATHOLIC VIEWER'S GUIDE

VERONICA BURCHARD

SOPHIA INSTITUTE PRESS
Manchester, NH

Printed in the United States of America
Cover and book design: Perceptions Design Studio.

SOPHIA
INSTITUTE PRESS

Box 5284, Manchester, NH 03108
1-800-888-9344
www.SophiaInstitute.com

Sophia Institute Press® is a registered trademark of Sophia Institute.

Library of Congress Cataloging-in-Publication Data

Burchard, Veronica, author.

A.D. Catholic viewer's guide / by Veronica Burchard.

pages cm

ISBN 978-1-62282-267-6 (pbk. : alk. paper) 1. Church history–Primitive and early church, ca. 30-600–Textbooks. 2. Bible. Acts–Miscellanea. 3. A.D. (Television program) I. A.D. (Television program) II. Title.

BR168.B87 2015

270.1–dc23   2015000802

TABLE OF CONTENTS

CATHOLIC
VIEWER'S GUIDE

HOW TO USE THIS GUIDE

A.D. The Bible Continues is based on the Holy Bible and strives to be true to its spirit. Certain characters and events are dramatizations.

This book contains a viewing guide for each episode of the *A.D.* series. We have offered a "Catholic takeaway," or key Catholic principle, for each episode. Keep this principle in mind as you prepare for, watch, and discuss each one.

In addition, each episode viewing guide contains:

- A short list of key events in the episode
- Map and timeline
- Important characters
- A short background reading
- Terms to know
- Biblical touchstone
- Connections to Scripture and writings of the saints
- Focus question
- Discussion questions
- Suggestions for evangelization
- Closing prayer

Important: If you don't want to know what happens, don't read ahead!

Note: A.D. The Bible Continues features a mix of historical and fictional characters. Even the words and actions of characters who have a biblical basis are often dramatizations. To learn more about the lives and sacrifices of those first Christians given the task of spreading the Gospel, read *Ministers and Martyrs: The Ultimate Catholic Guide to the Apostolic Age*, along with the *Holy Bible* and the *Catechism of the Catholic Church*.

In the Aftermath of the Crucifixion

33	46	64	71-80
Death of Christ	St. Paul's First Missionary Journey	Persecution of Christians Begins	Coliseum Built

IN THIS EPISODE

- Jesus suffers and dies on the Cross.
- Peter struggles with his guilt at having denied Jesus.
- Pilate releases Jesus' body to St. Joseph of Arimathea for burial.
- Caiaphas and Rome place guards at the tomb.

CITY OF JERUSALEM

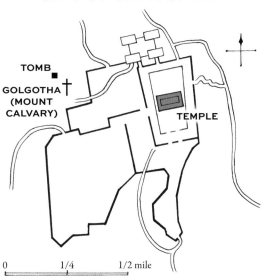

TOMB
GOLGOTHA (MOUNT CALVARY)
TEMPLE

0   1/4   1/2 mile

KEY CHARACTERS

Jesus Christ is God the Son, who became man to be with us. He died for our sins, and because of His sacrifice, heaven is open to us.

Blessed Virgin Mary is the Mother of Jesus. She stayed with Jesus throughout His agony on the Cross and never wavered in her faith in His promises.

Joseph Caiaphas is the Jewish high priest. He organized the plot to kill Jesus and sent Him to Pilate for His execution.

St. Joseph of Arimathea is a wealthy Israelite and a member of the Sanhedrin. He requested Jesus' body from Pilate and laid Him in his own tomb.

St. Mary of Magdala is a disciple of Christ. She was present at Christ's Crucifixion and Resurrection.

St. Peter is head of the Apostles. He was racked with guilt after his denial of Jesus and his failure to remain with Him through His suffering on the Cross.

Pontius Pilate is the prefect of the Roman province of Judea. He presided over Jesus' trial and agreed to release Jesus' body to St. Joseph of Arimathea.

THE CATHOLIC TAKEAWAY

Jesus' death and Resurrection remind us that we must die to self so that we may rise again as a new creation in Christ.

Understanding the Age

BY MIKE AQUILINA

Around 80,000 people lived in Jerusalem during the Roman occupation. Most of them were descendants of Israel. Most were Jews, and they knew that their city would be the site of the climactic scenes of the greatest drama in human history — a drama not merely of local importance, but cosmic in scale.

All Signs Point to Jerusalem

Jerusalem's residents knew this because the ancient prophets had foretold the events in some detail. Contemporary sages looked at the circumstances of that century, and they saw the telltale pattern of God's guidance. They expected God to intervene with power, vindicating His people and establishing a Kingdom. They imagined it taking place, as revolutions often do, with armed battles. The scenarios varied, depending upon the sage, but all agreed upon the importance of Jerusalem.

God launched His creation, the rabbis said, with Jerusalem — more precisely, with the foundation stone of Jerusalem's Temple. Creation expanded outward from that spot, and God Himself marked time from that moment. The stone marked the center of the earth and the focal point of true religion. In the Temple of King Solomon, the Ark of the Covenant rested on it.

When history came to its climax, it was indeed in Jerusalem. It came, however, not in the way anyone expected it. It followed none of the scripts of the first-century pundits. Yet it exceeded them all in the perfection of its fulfillment.

The salvation won by Jesus, the Messiah, arrived in stunning continuity with all the history that had gone before. And all subsequent history takes its reference from His redeeming work. Apart from Him, history is a futile and meaningless pursuit.

> The salvation won by Jesus, the Messiah, arrived in stunning continuity with all the history that had gone before. And all subsequent history takes its reference from His redeeming work. Apart from Him, history is a futile and meaningless pursuit.

Biblical religion is not mythology. It is historical. It takes place in a land that can be visited and explored. Its milestone events were recorded by witnesses whose testimony has been carefully preserved.

Christianity and History

History matters to Christians, as it mattered to the people of Jerusalem two millennia ago. The saving events are more important, in the grand scheme and in individual lives, than the wars that are fought today and the news that occupies our media. If we are to understand our lives, we must begin by understanding that long-ago moment in history.

What was the rock — the new foundation stone — on which Jesus said He would establish His new creation, new people, and new worship?

As we begin to explore the life of the early Church, we take our stand on firm ground, the solid rock of history. We stand with a curious historical figure and unlikely hero. His name is Simon Peter.

To learn more about the lives and sacrifices of those first Christians given the task of spreading the gospel, read *Ministers and Martyrs: The Ultimate Catholic Guide to the Apostolic Age.*

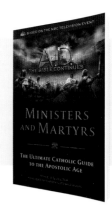

TERMS TO KNOW

- **Holy of Holies:** The inner sanctuary in the Jewish Temple. It was covered by a veil and originally contained the Ark of the Covenant. Only the high priest could enter this space.

- **Suffering Servant:** Isaiah 53:9 prophesied a mysterious suffering servant. Jesus Christ fulfilled this prophecy in multiple ways, including: "He was given a grave among the wicked, a burial place with evildoers, though he had done no wrong, nor was deceit found in his mouth."

- **Nazarene:** A person from the town of Nazareth in Galilee — the town where Jesus Christ grew up.

- **The Passover:** The commemoration of the Jewish people's deliverance from slavery in ancient Egypt.

- **Prefect:** The governor of a region. Pontius Pilate was the prefect of the Roman province of Judea.

- **Sanhedrin:** The ancient Jewish council of justice, made up of an assembly of men appointed in every city in Israel.

- **Zealot:** a member of an ancient Jewish sect favoring armed resistance against the Romans.

BIBLICAL TOUCHSTONE

To prepare to watch the episode, read one or more of the Gospel accounts of the Passion of our Lord. As you read, note what each author emphasizes in his account:

- **Matthew 26-27**
  Matthew emphasizes His Kingship. Why?

- **Mark 14-15**
  How does Mark show us the suffering of Jesus?

- **Luke 22-23**
  In what ways does Luke emphasize His innocence?

- **John 18-19**
  How does John assure us that Jesus willingly entered into His Passion and did the will of the Father?

SCRIPTURE AND THE SAINTS

John 19:34
"But one soldier thrust his lance into his side, and immediately blood and water flowed out."

The moment when blood and water poured from the open side of Jesus was the moment when the Church — the Bride of Christ — was born. Our new life in the Church was born out of Jesus' side after His death. This recalls how God made Adam's bride from his side while he slept. The water that flowed from the side of Jesus reminds us of the cleansing waters of Baptism, and the Blood is the Blood of the new Covenant, which is poured out for many for the forgiveness of sins. (See Gen. 2:21, Mt. 26:27-28, and 1 Cor. 15.)

 Did you know?
At every Mass, when the priest prepares the bread and wine that will become the Body and Blood of Jesus Christ, he also pours water into the chalice to reflect the blood and water that poured out of Jesus' side.

 Romans 6:4
"We were buried therefore with him by baptism into death, so that as Christ was raised from the dead by the glory of the Father, we too might walk in newness of life."

Christ's death and Resurrection remind us that we must die to self so that we may rise again in new life.

 St. Thomas Aquinas
"By the passion of Christ we acquire a complete cleansing from our sins and stains. ... And so it is these two things which are especially associated with two sacraments: water with the sacrament of baptism, and blood with the Eucharist."

FOCUS QUESTION

Jesus suffered and died so that we could have eternal life. As Catholics, we know we must die to self in order to live a new life in Christ. But we are not simply "born again" once. We must continually turn away from sin and seek God's mercy throughout our lives. What are some ways we do this?

DISCUSSION QUESTIONS

1. During His trial, Jesus offers very little in the way of defending Himself. Do you think this is how many in the crowd would have expected the Messiah to behave? What does this teach us about who Christ is and how Christians should act?

2. Why do you think Jesus willingly endured His suffering and death? Why would He not have just come down from the Cross?

3. St. Peter denied Jesus three times, just as Jesus had predicted he would. Why do you think Jesus gave St. Peter such an important role among the Apostles, even when He knew Peter would seem to abandon Him in the end?

4. Was Pontius Pilate evil? Explain why or why not.

5. Why was the veil of the Temple torn in two when Jesus died on the Cross and the Temple later destroyed?

ANALYZING THE EPISODE

PILATE: Are you the king of the Jews?

JESUS: My kingdom is not of this world . . .

PILATE: You are a king then?

JESUS: You say that I am. . . . I was born and came into this world to testify to the truth. Everyone on the side of the truth listens to me.

PILATE: Truth? What is truth?

Compare the account in the episode with the Gospel accounts in Matthew 27:11, Mark 15:2, Luke 23:3, and John 18:33-37.

GO FORTH AND EVANGELIZE

Near the end of the episode, Boaz tries to convince Peter to aggressively resist Roman rule. Boaz warns him, "They will snuff out His ideas one by one — until it will be as if they, He, and you never existed." In the days and years following Christ's Crucifixion, the responsibility to bring His message to others — to make disciples of all nations, as He had commanded them — was an especially urgent one. Had it not been for the courage and fortitude of the disciples, His message, and even the truth of His existence, might have been lost to the world forever.

Twenty centuries have come and gone. Have our responsibilities changed?

Read the quotation from St. Teresa of Ávila and then **add your own ideas** to the list of things you can do this week to be Christ's body, hands, and feet.

St. Teresa of Ávila
"Christ has no body now on earth but yours, no hands but yours.... Yours are the feet with which he is to go about doing good. Yours are the hands with which he is to bless men now."

BE CHRIST'S BODY

- Go to Confession, and receive the Eucharist at Holy Mass.

- Have a Mass said for a loved one who has died. Pray for the souls in Purgatory.

- Share with others the necessity of Baptism in the Christian life.

- If you are married, re-commit yourself to your marriage vows.

- Go out of your way to welcome people who are new to your area, school, or parish.

- Give up an "extra" treat you enjoy and give the money you saved to a charity that serves the poor.

- _____
  _____

- _____
  _____

BE CHRIST'S HANDS

- Bring meals to people who are sick, grieving, or unemployed.
- Prepare food and feed the hungry at a local soup kitchen.
- Donate warm clothing and mittens to a homeless shelter.
- Reach out and offer a hug to someone who is sad.

- Do repairs, yard work, and housework for an elderly person in your family or at a senior center.
- _____ _____
- _____ _____

BE CHRIST'S FEET

- Carry the message of Christ with you wherever you go.
- Visit people who are sick.
- Offer to do errands and help out in other ways.
- Donate time and resources to a crisis pregnancy center.
- Donate books to the imprisoned.

- Offer to drive friends to Mass and Confession.
- Pray and ask God for guidance in all you do.
- _____ _____
- _____ _____

CLOSING PRAYER

The _Anima Christi_ (Latin for "Soul of Christ") is a fourteenth-century prayer that gives us the opportunity to reflect on the Passion of our Lord. Attributed to St. Ignatius of Loyola, this prayer is often said after receiving Holy Communion, but it is appropriate to say anytime we want to ask Jesus to calm and guide us.

Soul of Christ, sanctify me.
Body of Christ, save me.
Blood of Christ, inebriate me.
Water from the side of Christ, wash me.
Passion of Christ, strengthen me.
O Good Jesus, hear me.
Within your wounds hide me.
Permit me not to be separated from you.
From the wicked foe, defend me.
At the hour of my death, call me and bid me come to you
That with your saints I may praise you forever and ever.
AMEN.

EPISODE 2
Christ Is Risen

33
Christ Rises
from the
Dead

46
St. Paul's First
Missionary
Journey

64
Persecution
of Christians
Begins

71-80
Coliseur
Built

IN THIS EPISODE

- The disciples are overjoyed when the risen Jesus returns to them.

- St. Thomas struggles with doubt.

- Forty days after the Resurrection, Jesus ascends into heaven.

- Jesus promises that He will pour out the Holy Spirit on the Apostles, who will be strengthened to preach the gospel to all nations.

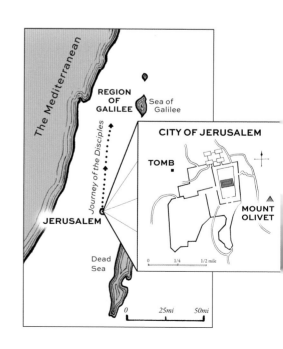

KEY CHARACTERS

 Jesus Christ is God the Son, who became man to be with us. He died for our sins and rose again on the third day in accordance with the Scriptures. He ascended into heaven and is seated at the right hand of the Father.

 Cornelius is a Roman centurion, the lieutenant of Pontius Pilate. His character has a biblical basis but is mostly fictionalized for the series. *For more information on the biblical Cornelius, see "Terms to Know" on page 106.*

 St. John is one of the twelve Apostles. Known as "the beloved disciple," St. John is overjoyed when St. Mary of Magdala tells him and St. Peter that Christ has been raised from the dead.

 St. Matthew is one of the twelve Apostles. A Jew, he worked for the Romans as a tax collector before becoming a disciple of Christ.

 "Reuben" is the right-hand man of Caiaphas, the Jewish high priest. He is fictionalized for the series. Caiaphas sends him to find Jesus' body.

 St. Simon is one of the twelve Apostles. He is called Simon the Zealot because of his strict adherence to Jewish and Canaanite law.

 St. Thomas is one of the twelve Apostles. He struggles with doubt about Christ's Resurrection until he is able to see and touch Jesus for himself.

 ## THE CATHOLIC TAKEAWAY

Faith is impossible without grace and the help of the Holy Spirit, but we also must use our intellects and our free will to cooperate with God's grace.

Apostle: One Who Is Sent

BY MIKE AQUILINA

The word *apostle* has a dynamic quality. The Greek *apostolos* means "one who is sent." It describes an agent or vicar, an emissary or ambassador. More than a messenger, an apostolos is a representative. Scholars believe the word is a direct translation of the Hebrew *shaliah*; and the ancient rabbis pronounced that "a man's shaliah is as himself."

The Apostles were first known as the Twelve — a number rich with meaning. For a Jew of the first century, it recalled the twelve tribes of Israel, the tribes now dispersed among the Gentiles and assimilated into other peoples. The gathering of the scattered was seen as an essential component of God's salvation. The reconstitution of Israel was a work expected of the Messiah, the Christ.

Jesus' choice of twelve leaders was symbolic and suggestive — even provocative. Clearly he sensed the gravity of the moment. He spent the preceding night in a vigil of intense prayer.

It is unlikely that the Apostles themselves would have missed the significance of their number. Jesus himself stated it explicitly as He turned the kingdom over to them at His Last Supper: "You are those who have continued with me in my trials; and I assign to you, as my Father assigned to me, a kingdom, that you may eat and drink at my table in my kingdom, and sit on thrones judging the twelve tribes of Israel" (Luke 22:28-30).

As Jesus transferred authority to the Apostles, He compared the action to His own commissioning by God the Father: "As the Father has sent me, even so I send you" (John 20:21). As Jesus had acted in the power of the Holy Spirit, so He gave the Spirit in turn to His chosen men (John 20:22).

The office of Apostle was not something any of the Twelve had earned. They had, in fact, repeatedly proven themselves unworthy of the office

> It is remarkable to see the certainty and confidence with which the Apostles established the life that the Church would follow ever afterward. Jesus gave them the Great Commission to take the Gospel to "all nations." And they were faithful to the command.

and unprepared for the tasks. After years of instruction, they could still move their Teacher to exasperation: "Have I been with you so long, and yet you do not know me?" (John 14:9). In the face of danger, they had "scattered," running to their homes, leaving Christ "alone" (John 16:32).

The Apostles themselves knew their unworthiness; but they also knew the dignity of their office. Paul spoke of the inner circle of Peter, John, and James as "pillars" of the Church (Gal. 2:9). The Twelve were the "foundation" Paul was building on, while Christ was the "cornerstone" (Eph. 2:20). In the book of Revelation, John sees the Twelve enshrined as foundation stones of the new and heavenly Jerusalem (Rev. 21:14).

It is remarkable — considering their failures recorded in the Gospels — to see the certainty and confidence with which the Apostles established the life that the Church would follow ever afterward. Jesus gave them the Great Commission to take the Gospel to "all nations" (Mt. 28:19), "to the end of the earth" (Acts 1:8). And they were faithful to the command. Peter and Paul traveled westward to Rome; Thomas eastward to India; others to Armenia, Persia, Greece — everywhere laying foundations for the Church as we know it today.

To learn more about the lives and sacrifices of those first Christians given the task of spreading the gospel, read *Ministers and Martyrs: The Ultimate Catholic Guide to the Apostolic Age.*

TERMS TO KNOW

- **Mikvah:** A bath used for ritual immersion and purification in Orthodox Judaism.

- **Roman seal:** Roman guards placed a soft, moldable substance (probably clay) imprinted with the Roman imperial symbol on the enormous and heavy rock covering Jesus' tomb. The seal was an extra security measure to prevent the theft of Jesus' body.

- **Upper Room:** According to tradition, the Upper Room was a large chamber in a house in Jerusalem near the present Zion Gate and the Armenian quarter. Frequently used as a meeting place, the Upper Room was the site of the Last Supper and the descent of the Holy Spirit at Pentecost.

BIBLICAL TOUCHSTONE

Read the scriptural accounts of the Ascension in Luke 24:50-53, Mark 16:19, and Acts 1:9-11. Then pray a decade of the Scriptural Rosary, meditating on the Second Glorious Mystery: the Ascension.

OUR FATHER ...

"Then he led them [out] as far as Bethany, raised his hands, and blessed them." (Luke 24:50)

HAIL MARY ...

"Then Jesus approached and said to them, 'All power in heaven and on earth has been given to me.'"
(Mt. 28:18)

HAIL MARY ...

"'Go, therefore, and make disciples of all nations, baptizing them in the name of the Father, and of the Son, and of the holy Spirit, teaching them to observe all that I have commanded you.'" (Mt. 28:19-20)

HAIL MARY ...

"'And behold, I am with you always, until the end of the age.'" (Mt. 28:20)

HAIL MARY ...

"'Whoever believes and is baptized will be saved; whoever does not believe will be condemned.'" (Mark 16:16)

HAIL MARY ...

"As he blessed them he parted from them and was taken up to heaven." (Luke 24:51)

HAIL MARY ...

"He was lifted up, and a cloud took him from their sight." (Acts 1:9)

HAIL MARY ...

"'This Jesus who has been taken up from you into heaven will return in the same way as you have seen him going into heaven.'" (Acts 1:11)

HAIL MARY ...

"They did him homage and then returned to Jerusalem with great joy." (Luke 24:52)

HAIL MARY ...

"Jesus ... took his seat at the right hand of God." (Mark 16:19)

HAIL MARY ...

SCRIPTURE AND THE SAINTS

> **Hebrews 11:1**
> "Faith is the realization of what is hoped for and evidence of things not seen."

Faith seeks understanding. We have a natural and good desire to understand God and His promises to humanity. Sometimes our world with all its troubles, injustice, and suffering can seem very different from the one God promises us, and it can be tempting to lose faith. When this happens, we can look to the examples of Abraham, Noah, St. Joseph, the Virgin Mary, and others whose faith remained steadfast even when put to the test. We can ask God to help us trust in Him, just like the father in the Gospel of Mark who cried out, "I do believe, help my unbelief!" after Jesus told him that "everything is possible to one who has faith." (Mark 9:23-24).

 Did you know?
The third time the risen Jesus revealed Himself to the Apostles mirrors His first call to the disciples. Both times the fishermen doubted at first, but their nets soon overflowed with fish.

 St. Thomas Aquinas
"Believing is an act of the intellect assenting to the divine truth by command of the will moved by God through grace."

 St. Anselm
"I do not seek to understand in order that I may believe, but I believe in order to understand. For this also I believe: that unless I believe I shall not understand."

FOCUS QUESTION

Christ invites us to believe in Him, but He never forces anyone to have faith. The Church teaches that faith is a free and unmerited gift of God and also that "man's response to God by faith must be free.... The act of faith is of its very nature a free act" (*Dignitatis Humanae* 10). What are some ways in which we can cooperate with God's grace to increase our faith?

DISCUSSION QUESTIONS

1. In this episode, many characters struggle to understand what has happened. Others struggle to believe. In what ways can we seek to strengthen our ability both to believe and to understand God's Word and our Catholic Faith?

2. If you had been there, how do you think you would have reacted to the news that Jesus was risen? Would you have responded like the Virgin Mary, like St. Peter, or like St. Thomas?

3. In what ways does the Blessed Virgin Mary most perfectly embody the obedience of faith?

4. The third time the risen Jesus revealed Himself to His disciples, He had a conversation with Peter in which He asked Peter three times if he loved Him. Why do you think Jesus did this?

5. Jesus also told Peter three times to feed and tend His flock. Why did He tell these things to Peter in particular?

ANALYZING THE EPISODE

JESUS: Put your finger here and see my hands, and bring your hand and put it into my side, and do not be unbelieving, but believe.

THOMAS: My Lord and my God!

JESUS: Have you come to believe because you have seen me? Blessed are those who have not seen and have believed.

The scene in which St. Thomas encounters the risen Jesus is described in the Gospel of John. Read John 20:27-29 and ask the Holy Spirit to strengthen your own faith.

GO FORTH AND EVANGELIZE

At the Ascension, Jesus told the disciples: "But you will receive power when the Holy Spirit comes upon you, and you will be my witnesses in Jerusalem, throughout Judea and Samaria, and to the ends of the earth" (Acts 1:8). Matthew's Gospel tells us that He commanded the Apostles, "Go, therefore, and make disciples of all nations" (Mt. 28:19).

Like the Apostles, we too are called to bring the Good News to others. Christ ascended into heaven, but He is still here with us, and He sends the Holy Spirit to strengthen us in the task. We can rely on the theological virtues — faith, hope, and love — to be united with Christ and bring His saving message to all.

In his Homily on the Ascension, St. Augustine said, "Why do we on earth not strive to find rest with Him in heaven even now, through the faith, hope, and love that unite us to Him? While in heaven he is also with us; and we while on earth are with Him. He is here with us by His divinity, His power and His love. We cannot be in heaven, as He is on earth, by divinity, but in Him, we can be there by love."

This week, let the theological virtues guide you in your mission to evangelize. Add your own ideas to the list below.

FAITH

- Offer an Act of Faith in your daily prayers.
- Tell a friend who is going through a difficult time that you are praying for her, and ask what you can do to help.

- _____
  _____
- _____
  _____

HOPE

- Invite a friend to pray a decade of the Rosary with you. Together, meditate on the Ascension and pray for the spiritual fruit of hope.
- Donate good books to the imprisoned, or make a donation to a charity that does this.

- _____
  _____
- _____
  _____

LOVE

- Practice the Spiritual Works of Mercy.
- If you are married, never let a day go by without telling your spouse that you love him/her.

- _____
  _____
- _____
  _____

CLOSING PRAYER

Though we are often like St. Thomas, struggling with our faith, let us pray to be more like the Blessed Virgin Mary, who never wavered in her belief in the fulfillment of God's Word.

This Prayer for Faith comes to us from Pope Paul VI. In this prayer, we ask the Lord to increase our faith and make us more joyful, humble, and docile in our obedience to Christ and His one holy, catholic, and apostolic Church.

Prayer for Faith

Lord, I believe:
I wish to believe in Thee.
Lord, let my faith be full
and unreserved,
and let it penetrate my thought,
my way of judging Divine things
and human things.
Lord, let my faith be joyful
and give peace and gladness
to my spirit,
and dispose it for prayer with God
and conversation with men,
so that the inner bliss of its

fortunate possession
may shine forth in sacred
and secular conversation.
Lord, let my faith be humble
and not presume
to be based on the experience of
my thought and of my feeling;
but let it surrender to the testimony
of the Holy Spirit,
and not have any better guarantee
than in docility to Tradition
and to the authority of the Magisterium
of the Holy Church.

AMEN.

EPISODE 3
Come, Holy Spirit

33
Holy Spirit Descends at
Pentecost, Fifty Days
after Death of Christ

33
Christ Rises
from the
Dead

46
St. Paul's First
Missionary
Journey

64
Persecution
of Christians
Begins

71-80
Coliseu
Built

IN THIS EPISODE

- The arrival of the Holy Spirit at Pentecost marks the birthday of the Church.

- Filled with the gifts of the Holy Spirit, the Apostles come out of hiding and begin to preach the gospel.

- Peter is arrested following his miraculous healing of a beggar.

- Caiaphas and Pilate struggle to contain the news of the Resurrection, and Pilate's life is threatened.

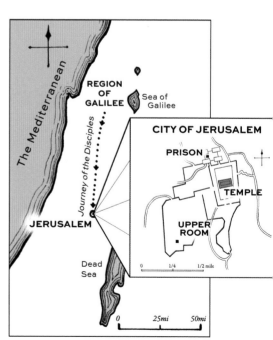

KEY CHARACTERS

 Herod Antipas is the tetrarch of Galilee (a tetrarch was a ruler of a principality). Unlike his father, Herod I the Great, Antipas displayed sensitivity to his Jewish subjects.

 "Boaz" is a zealot who plans to assassinate Pontius Pilate at the festival of Pentecost. His character is fictionalized for the series.

 "Claudia" is the wife of Pontius Pilate. With the exception of her dream that warned that her husband should have nothing to do with Jesus, her character is fictionalized for the series. She worries for her husband's safety but is also concerned that he isn't being completely honest with her. *See "Terms to Know" on page 28 for more information.*

 "Leah" is the wife of Caiaphas, the Jewish high priest. Her character has a historical basis in that Caiaphas was in fact married to the daughter of Annas, the former high priest. Leah schemes to protect her husband from harm.

 "Maya" is St. Peter's daughter, fictionalized for the series. St. Peter might have had a daughter, St. Petronilla, but she was likely a spiritual "daughter" converted by St. Peter rather than his biological child.

 Melek is the name given to the crippled beggar who is miraculously healed by St. Peter in Acts 3.

 ## THE CATHOLIC TAKEAWAY

The Holy Spirit is the Giver of Life, and we can ask for and receive His help to do what the Apostles did: proclaim that Jesus Christ is Lord.

The Great Harvest of Pentecost

BY MIKE AQUILINA

Pentecost was the annual harvest festival of the Jews, and it was one of three feasts that all Jewish males were bound by law to observe in the holy city (Exod. 23:14-17). In Hebrew the day was Shavuot, the Feast of Weeks, because it took place on the day following a "week of weeks" — seven times seven days — counting from Passover (Lev. 23:15-16). Originally a harvest festival, the feast was a ritual reminder that God was the source of Israel's blessings — that they owed their first and best of everything to Him.

Over the centuries, Pentecost had grown in importance, and it had gathered layers of spiritual and historical significance. By the time of Jesus and the Apostles, it had become primarily a celebration of the giving of the law to Moses, a completion of Passover. What God had begun in Egypt, He sealed by the giving of the law at Sinai.

The Apostles were living in expectation. Jesus had told them "to wait for the promise of the Father. . . . You shall be baptized with the Holy Spirit. . . . You shall receive power when the Holy Spirit has come upon you" (see Acts 1:4-8).

During the forty days after Passover — the forty days after His Resurrection — Jesus appeared to the Apostles and taught them. Yet he trained their gaze forward in time, as if His work was not yet done, as if His Passover awaited its completion.

> A sound came from heaven like the rush of a mighty wind. Tongues of fire appeared and rested on the disciples. The Holy Spirit arrived in a great show of power, attended by amazing wonders, manifest before a cast of thousands.

Pentecost is indeed the setting of the most spectacular scene in the historical books of the New Testament. A sound came from heaven like the rush of a mighty wind. Tongues of fire appeared and rested on the disciples — but did not burn them! The men rushed into the streets and began to proclaim Jesus Christ before the multitude that had gathered in Jerusalem for the feast day. The Holy Spirit arrived in a great show of power, attended by amazing wonders, manifest before a cast of thousands.

Pilgrims had come to Jerusalem from all the nations of the world. They

heard Peter preach the gospel and were converted. The means were now in place for the message to reach the farthest corners of Earth. It would be universal in scope. It would be catholic.

As God had once given the law to Moses, so now He gave His own Spirit to the Church. The Spirit was manifest in unexpected prodigies and charisms (from the Greek word for "gifts") — such as speaking in diverse tongues and understanding those tongues. Mere men were entrusted with the means of salvation, a divine action. Among those charisms was the gift of leadership, *authority*. It is significant that not everyone preached on the first Pentecost; not everyone led; not everyone taught; not everyone issued the call to repentance. Peter did; the Apostles did. They fulfilled the roles of the office they had been given by Jesus.

Some years before, Jesus had said to his disciples, "The harvest is plentiful" (Luke 10:2). And the great harvest began, appropriately enough, at Pentecost, the feast of the harvest — the day dedicated to the gathering and offering of firstfruits.

To learn more about the lives and sacrifices of those first Christians given the task of spreading the gospel, read *Ministers and Martyrs: The Ultimate Catholic Guide to the Apostolic Age.*

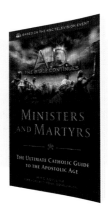

TERMS TO KNOW

- **Pentecost:** Meaning "fiftieth," Pentecost was a Jewish festival celebrated fifty days after Passover. Fifty days after His death, Jesus poured out the Holy Spirit on the Apostles and the Church. Whereas before they were afraid and in hiding, after Pentecost the Apostles were filled with fortitude. They were willing to endure beatings, imprisonment, and, later, martyrdom, for their mission. On Pentecost Peter gave a wonderful sermon, and thousands were converted. For these reasons, Pentecost is celebrated as the birthday of the Church.

- **Tetrarch:** A Roman tetrarch was the ruler of a quarter of a region or province. After the death of Herod the Great, his region was ruled by his three sons, including Herod Antipas, tetrarch of Galilee.

- **"Claudia":** The name given in some traditions to the wife of Pontius Pilate. Pilate's wife is unnamed in the New Testament and mentioned only a single time in the Gospel of Matthew: "While [Pilate] was still seated on the bench, his wife sent him a message, 'Have nothing to do with that righteous man. I suffered much in a dream today because of him'" (Mt. 27:19). Pilate's wife is honored as St. Claudia Procles in the Eastern Orthodox and Ethiopian Orthodox Churches.

BIBLICAL TOUCHSTONE

Read chapters 2 and 3 of the Acts of the Apostles. As you read, take note of the major events and reflect on how all of them were central to the birthday of the Church.

- **The Coming of the Spirit (Acts 2:1-13)**
- **Peter's speech at Pentecost (Acts 2:14-36)**
- **Baptism of the faithful (Acts 2:37-41)**
- **Communal life: signs and wonders, and breaking bread (Acts 2:41-47)**
- **Peter's cure of the crippled beggar (Acts 3:1-10)**
- **Peter's speech (Acts 3:11-26)**

SCRIPTURE AND THE SAINTS

Romans 8:26

"In the same way, the Spirit too comes to the aid of our weakness; for we do not know how to pray as we ought, but the Spirit itself intercedes with inexpressible groanings."

We are all temples of the Holy Spirit — the Giver of Life. The one, holy, catholic, and apostolic Church was born of the Holy Spirit on Pentecost. As the Holy Spirit breathed life into the Church, we can also receive the Holy Spirit into our own lives. If Peter and the Apostles had relied on themselves to know what to say and do, they would surely have failed. It was only when they received the Holy Spirit and became docile and obedient to the Lord that they were filled with the courage and strength to proclaim the Good News.

 Did you know?

The word *spirit* comes from the Latin *inspirare*, which means to enflame or to blow into. It is fitting that Jesus breathed on the Apostles when He told them to receive the Holy Spirit (John 20:22) and that tongues of fire enflamed the Apostles at Pentecost (Acts 2:3).

 St. Josemaría Escríva

"The Apostles, though they had been taught by Jesus for three years, fled in terror from the enemies of Christ. But after Pentecost they let themselves be flogged and imprisoned, and ended up giving their lives in witness to their faith."

 John 15:5

"I am the vine, you are the branches. Whoever remains in me and I in him will bear much fruit, because without me you can do nothing."

FOCUS QUESTION

The Holy Spirit prepares us and stays with us when we speak and act to bring others to Christ. How can we be open to receiving the Holy Spirit's help? What examples can we learn from the Apostles?

DISCUSSION QUESTIONS

1. Peter can't help worrying that Jesus picked the wrong man to lead His Church. Why do you think he felt that way?

2. Does Peter act like a leader — indeed, like the first Pope — on Pentecost Sunday?

3. What was the Virgin Mary's role at Pentecost? What does this tell us about the role of the Virgin Mary in the life of the Church?

4. At Pentecost, some who observed the disciples thought they were drunk: "But others said, scoffing, 'They have had too much new wine'" (Acts 2:13). Other than actual wine, what else might "new wine" refer to in this passage?

5. The Apostles received the gifts of the Holy Spirit at Pentecost. How do their actions following the Descent of the Holy Spirit show wisdom, understanding, counsel, fortitude, knowledge, piety, and fear of the Lord?

ANALYZING THE EPISODE

PETER: Look at us, we have no money, no silver, no gold. But what I have I give you. In the name of Jesus of Nazareth, rise up and walk.

After receiving the Holy Spirit, Peter performs the first of several miraculous healings. Read Matthew 10:8.

- **What command does Christ give?**

- **To whom does He give it?**

- **How does Peter obey this command in this scene?**

- **How do priests today follow this command of Christ?**

GO FORTH AND EVANGELIZE

As faithful Christians, we are called to do what the Blessed Virgin Mary and the Apostles did at Pentecost — proclaim the New Covenant. And just like Sts. Peter and John in this episode, we too may face hostility and even violence for sharing Christ with others. This week, make it a special mission to do what the Apostles did: pray for, receive, and act on the gifts of the Holy Spirit. These virtues are of special importance for evangelists.

Some ideas are listed below. What would you add?

WISDOM

- Select and read a spiritual self-help book together with a friend.

- _____
  _____

- _____
  _____

- _____
  _____

UNDERSTANDING

- Pray, as St. Paul did, "May the eyes of [your] hearts be enlightened, that you may know what is the hope that belongs to his call, what are the riches of glory in his inheritance among the holy ones" (Eph. 1:18).

- _____
  _____

- _____
  _____

COUNSEL

- Serve as a Confirmation sponsor to a young Catholic or an adult in RCIA.

- _____
  _____

- _____
  _____

FORTITUDE

- Fight against injustice and help those who are vulnerable. Join a pro-life group, donate to help persecuted Christians in the Middle East, and look for other ways to be a peacemaker.

- _____
_____

- _____
_____

KNOWLEDGE

- Speak the truth with charity, even when the truth is unpopular.

- _____
_____

- _____
_____

- _____
_____

PIETY

- Keep the commandments; love God and your neighbor.

- _____
_____

- _____
_____

- _____
_____

FEAR OF THE LORD

- Examine your conscience. Together with your child(ren), other family members, or friends, go to Confession before receiving Holy Communion at Mass on Sunday.

- _____
_____

- _____
_____

CLOSING PRAYER

The ancient prayer Come, Holy Spirit has roots in the Psalms, hymns of various liturgical traditions, and ninth-century prayer books.

In this prayer, we ask the Holy Spirit to enflame and enlighten us as the Apostles were by "tongues of fire" (Acts 2:3) at Pentecost and to help us receive and develop the wisdom and discernment always to do God's will.

Come, Holy Spirit, fill the hearts of Your faithful and enkindle in them the fire of Your love. Send forth Your Spirit and they shall be created. And You shall renew the face of the earth. O God, Who by the light of the Holy Spirit instructed the hearts of the faithful, grant that by the same Spirit we may know what is right and always rejoice in His consolation, through Christ our Lord.

AMEN.

If praying as a group:

Come, Holy Spirit, fill the hearts of Your faithful and enkindle in them the fire of Your love.

Leader: Send forth Your Spirit, and they shall be created.

Response: And You shall renew the face of the earth.

Let us pray.

O God, Who by the light of the Holy Spirit, did instruct the hearts of the faithful, grant that by the same Holy Spirit we may be truly wise and ever enjoy His consolations. Through Christ our Lord.

AMEN.

Signs and Wonders

33	46	64	71-80
Christ Rises from the Dead	St. Paul's First Missionary Journey	Persecution of Christians Begins	Coliseu Built

IN THIS EPISODE

- Peter and John are released from their trial.

- Christians are now beyond counting, and among the new converts is Stephen, a bold young man who is eager to start preaching in the Temple.

- A great fear comes upon the whole Church when two new converts, Ananias and Sapphira, are struck down by God.

- Pilate starts crucifying civilians daily until the assassin is exposed.

CITY OF JERUSALEM

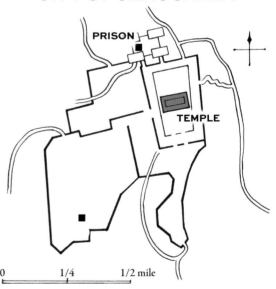

PRISON

TEMPLE

0   1/4   1/2 mile

KEY CHARACTERS

Ananias and Sapphira: A wealthy husband and wife who, like Barnabas, sell their land and give the proceeds to the Apostles. Unlike Barnabas, however, they lie about the sale price and secretly keep a portion of the money. The Bible tells us that upon this lie to God, Ananias "fell down and breathed his last" and Sapphira "fell down at [Peter's] feet and breathed her last" (Acts 5:5; 5:10).

St. Barnabas is a disciple who sells his property and gives the proceeds to the growing Christian community led by the Apostles. He was originally named Joseph, but Apostles rename him Barnabas, which means "Son of Encouragement."

St. John is one of the twelve Apostles. He is released from his trial when the crowd accepts the beggar's cure as miraculous.

Pontius Pilate is the prefect of the Roman province of Judea. Following the attempt on his life, he begins crucifying civilians daily until the assassin in exposed.

St. Peter is head of the Apostles. Once he is released from prison, he immediately goes back to work addressing the Christians.

St. Stephen is a newly baptized convert to the Faith. He is eager to begin preaching in the Temple but obeys when St. Peter tells him to be patient.

THE CATHOLIC TAKEAWAY

Love means total self-giving. Just as Jesus gave us His whole self, and the Apostles gave all for the mission Christ gave them, we too must give ourselves completely to those we love: God, our spouse, and our neighbors. Withholding is sin.

The Trinity

BY MIKE AQUILINA

In many places throughout the world, Christians observe Pentecost as a celebration of God as the Trinity — three divine persons living eternally in perfect unity: Father, Son, and Holy Spirit. The Trinity is the mystery at the heart of Christianity.

The Apostles' monotheism was continuous with their religious heritage. God had said through the prophet Isaiah: "I am the LORD, and there is no other, besides me there is no God" (Isa. 45:5). Yet from the first day of the Church's life, it was clear that the one God is also three. As Peter preached his first public sermon, he spoke of the Father, the Son, and the Spirit: "Being therefore exalted at the right hand of God, and having received from the Father the promise of the Holy Spirit, [Jesus] has poured out this which you see and hear" (Acts 2:33).

The God Peter preached was not a solitary being but an eternal communion. The God revealed on Pentecost was interpersonal. Only of such a deity could the Apostles say: "God is love" (1 John 4:8, 16).

The Apostles grounded this most fundamental belief in a revelation given by Jesus. In the last sentence recorded in St. Matthew's Gospel, Jesus instructed His disciples to baptize "in the name of the Father and of the Son and of the Holy Spirit" (Mt. 28:19). They were to act in one divine "name" that clearly applied to three distinct persons. Father, Son, and Spirit share the "name" of God equally. Jesus' Great Commission, then, was the immediate background for Peter's first proclamation.

Jesus showed the Apostles something that had previously been veiled from human sight, something humanity could not have discovered on its own. The Apsotles were duty-bound to report the content of the revelation, even though they could not pretend to comprehend it.

Christians, over time, would reflect on the mystery and see hints of it in the Old Testament — in God's use of first-person

> The God Peter preached was not a solitary being but an eternal communion. The God revealed on Pentecost was interpersonal. Only of such a deity could the Apostles say: "God is love" (1 John 4:8, 16).

plural pronouns such as *we, us,* and *our,* for example, and in the manifestation of three heavenly visitors to Abraham.

It is clear from the preaching of the Apostles that they considered Jesus and the Holy Spirit to be divine, yet distinct from one another. Paul pronounced blessings in Jesus' name (Rom. 16:20; 1 Cor. 16:23) and in the name of the Trinity: "The grace of the Lord Jesus Christ and the love of God and the fellowship of the Holy Spirit be with you all" (2 Cor. 13:14).

This revelation arrived as something more than mere "information." The experience of the Trinitarian God was decidedly new. The eternal Word had "pitched his tent" among His people; that's the literal meaning of the Greek in John 1:14. And, as if that were not close enough, He promised that they would share His life in a still deeper way. He would "abide" in them, and they would abide in Him (15:4-10). They would be "filled" with the Holy Spirit (Acts 2:4; 4:8; 6:3; 6:5; 7:55; 13:52).

To learn more about the lives and sacrifices of those first Christians given the task of spreading the gospel, read *Ministers and Martyrs: The Ultimate Catholic Guide to the Apostolic Age.*

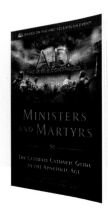

TERMS TO KNOW

- **Crucifixion:** A means of execution practiced in ancient Rome. This punishment was reserved for slaves, foreigners, and base criminals and was almost never inflicted on Roman citizens. Crucifixion was the agonizing death suffered by our Lord Jesus Christ.

- **Kaddish:** Often recited at funerals and by grieving family and friends, the Kaddish is a prayer in praise of God that expresses the mourner's longing for the establishment of God's kingdom on earth.

- **Sanhedrin:** The ancient Jewish council of justice, made up of an assembly of men appointed in every city in Israel.

- **Rock:** Peter is the rock on which Christ said He would build His Church. The Gospel of John tells of when our Lord gave Peter his new name — *Cephas* — which is an Anglicized form of the Aramaic word *Kepha*, which means "rock" (cf. John 1:42). In the Gospel of Matthew, Jesus tells Peter "And so I say to you, you are Peter, and upon this rock I will build my church. ... I will give you the keys to the kingdom of heaven. Whatever you bind on earth shall be bound in heaven; and whatever you loose on earth shall be loosed in heaven" (Mt. 16:18-19). Jesus gave Peter, as head of the Apostles, the authority to carry on His ministry and make binding decisions for the Church.

BIBLICAL TOUCHSTONE

Read chapter 4 of the Acts of the Apostles and reflect on the differences between St. Barnabas, on the one hand, and Ananias and Sapphira on the other. How do they differ in Christian virtues such as:

- **Faith**
- **Charity**
- **Total self-giving**
- **Honesty**

- **Understanding**
- **Fear of the Lord**
- **Realization of the seriousness of sin**

SCRIPTURE AND THE SAINTS

John 13:34

"I give you a new commandment: love one another. As I have loved you, so you also should love one another."

To love is to make a gift of oneself. God is love, and in Jesus Christ and the Holy Family, He has given us many beautiful examples of what it is to love. "The Church is born primarily of Christ's total self-giving for our salvation, anticipated in the institution of the Eucharist and fulfilled on the cross" (*Catechism of the Catholic Church* 766). While the Apostles gave all they had for Christ and His Church, we see in the example of Ananias and Sapphira the damaging effects of a false love that lies and withholds.

 Did you know?

Jesus said, "You shall love the Lord your God with all your heart, with all your soul, with all your mind, and with all your strength. . . . You shall love your neighbor as yourself.' There is no other commandment greater than these" (Mark 12:30-31). These commandments can be understood as a wonderful summary of the Ten Commandments.

 Matthew 16:24-25

"'Whoever wishes to come after me must deny himself, take up his cross, and follow me. For whoever wishes to save his life will lose it, but whoever loses his life for my sake will find it.'"

 St. Francis of Assisi

"Remember that when you leave this earth, you can take with you nothing that you have received — only what you have given."

FOCUS QUESTION

Pope Francis said, "Thinking that God is love does us so much good, because it teaches us to love, to give ourselves to others as Jesus gave himself to us and walks with us. Jesus walks beside us on the road through life." In what ways do you show love to God and your neighbor by giving of yourself?

DISCUSSION QUESTIONS

1. Why do you think the Holy Spirit is often depicted as a breath of wind?

2. Sts. Peter and John face a trial as Jesus did. How does their trial differ from the one Jesus endured?

3. It could seem that Jesus has caused trouble for St. Peter and the Apostles by revealing Himself to only a select few after His Resurrection. Why do you think He didn't make a public appearance to everyone in Jerusalem? To everyone in the world?

4. St. Stephen is brimming with excitement to preach in the Temple immediately. But St. Peter tells him to be patient, and Stephen obeys. What does their conversation show us about Peter's authority among Christians?

5. As news of St. Peter's miraculous healing spreads, the sick and the lame fill his path. What is the difference between Jesus' miraculous healings and Peter's?

ANALYZING THE EPISODE

CAIAPHAS: You are to be released. But it is on the condition that you do not speak, or teach, the name of Jesus of Nazareth. Break this condition, and you in turn will be broken.

PETER: You have judged us; now you must judge if in God's eyes it's right that we obey you rather than Him.

Read Acts 4:19. How have saints throughout history answered the demands of unjust rulers with similar fortitude?

GO FORTH AND EVANGELIZE

Blessed Mother Teresa said, "Intense love does not measure; it just gives." This week and always, make a special effort to give of yourself. Make sacrifices that are both material and spiritual.

Here are a few ideas — add your own ways that make use of your talents and interests.

- Spend an hour in adoration before the Blessed Sacrament.

-   _____
  _____
  _____

- Attend daily Mass, or resolve to go to Mass on First Fridays.

-   _____
  _____
  _____

- Bring a meal to a neighbor who is ill or who recently had a baby.

-   _____
  _____
  _____

- Organize a clothing drive for the needy.

-   _____
  _____
  _____

- Organize a schedule to bring meals to a homeless shelter or a soup kitchen.

- _____
  _____
  _____

- If you are married, give yourself completely to your spouse. Do not put any barriers between your total, mutual self-giving. Trust in God and be open to receiving new life.

- _____
  _____
  _____

CLOSING PRAYER

Throughout the Scriptures, simple and uneducated people like shepherds and fishermen have always discerned the truth before the kings and wise men did. During the trial of Peter and John, the Bible tells us that the crowd observed their boldness, and "perceiving them to be uneducated, ordinary men, they were amazed, and they recognized them as the companions of Jesus" (Acts 4:13).

This week, we will pray these words from St. John of the Cross to be open to receiving God's Word in all its beautiful simplicity and to give freely of ourselves the way Jesus did:

O Jesus, my Love, may my heart be consumed in loving Thee.

Make me humble and holy.

Give me childlike simplicity.

Transform me in thy holy love.

O Jesus, life of my life, joy of my soul, God of my heart, accept my heart as an altar, on which I will sacrifice to Thee the gold of ardent charity, the incense of continual, humble, and fervent prayer, and the myrrh of constant sacrifices! AMEN.

EPISODE 5
The Stoning of St. Stephen

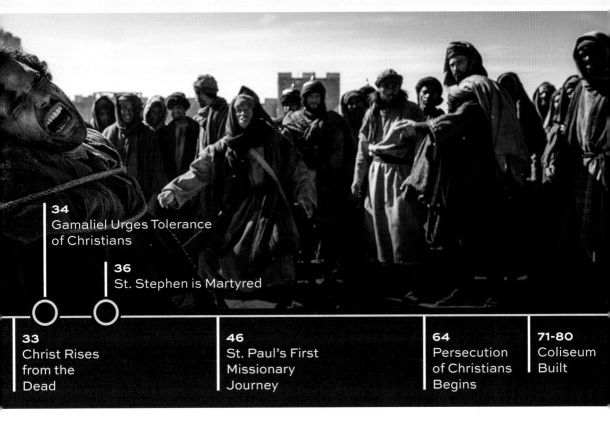

34
Gamaliel Urges Tolerance
of Christians

36
St. Stephen is Martyred

33
Christ Rises
from the
Dead

46
St. Paul's First
Missionary
Journey

64
Persecution
of Christians
Begins

71-80
Coliseum
Built

IN THIS EPISODE

- The Apostles are freed from captivity by an angel of the Lord.

- Wracked with guilt over the innocents who are dying in his place, Boaz turns himself in. Levi spares him from Roman torture with an arrow to the heart.

- The Apostles are arrested for preaching, but their punishment is reduced to flogging, thanks to the counsel of Gamaliel

- St. Stephen becomes the first martyr of the Church.

CITY OF JERUSALEM

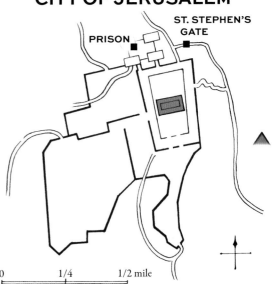

ST. STEPHEN'S
GATE

PRISON

0   1/4   1/2 mile

KEY CHARACTERS

 "Eva" is Boaz's fiancée, fictionalized for the series. Feeling guilty for her role in leading Caiaphas to Boaz, she asks Levi to teach her how to kill.

 Gamaliel, the head of the Sanhedrin, urges tolerance of Christians. Thanks to his advice, Caiaphas and the council spare the Apostles the death penalty when they are again arrested for preaching.

 "Levi" is one of Boaz's fellow zealots. He puts Boaz out of his misery while he is being tortured by the Romans. He is fictionalized for the series.

 St. James is one of the twelve Apostles and the brother of St. John.

 St. Peter is head of the Apostles. He and his fellow disciples are imprisoned, freed by an angel, and then imprisoned again when they immediately resume preaching.

 St. Stephen is a disciple of Christ and one of the first men to be ordained a deacon. He becomes the first martyr of the Church.

 **THE CATHOLIC TAKEAWAY**

As Christians, we are called to love our neighbor even when it's hard to do so.

The Rulers of Jesus' Time

BY MIKE AQUILINA

Both Pontius Pilate and Caiaphas were important men, respected and feared. Pilate was the Roman prefect in Judea, Caiaphas the high priest of the Jerusalem Temple. Both were accomplished men who had risen far in their chosen fields. They had to deal often with one another, negotiating a fragile peace and maintaining a difficult order in the land it was their lot to share. Each man seems to have had a measure of respect for the other and his people — oddly mixed with a measure of contempt.

The law dictated that the high priest, once ordained, should hold office for the remainder of his life. But during the dynasty of the Herods — and even their predecessors — the office of high priesthood had become a reward for political loyalty. King Herod the Great, who reigned when Jesus was born, installed and removed high priests at will, and some he murdered. By the time of Jesus' adulthood, the office went exclusively to candidates whom the ruling powers considered to be reliable.

A high priest should have been honored and should have wielded influence, but many religious Jews now viewed the office with contempt.

As the Romans took greater control of the region, they established a large military presence there and assigned a prefect to govern the people. The fifth man to hold that office was Pontius Pilate. Pilate could be brutal. He showed little sensitivity to Jewish customs, and it was he who made the fateful decision to move the Roman army from its pagan outpost to Jerusalem. With the army came images — on shields and banners — of Caesar and of the Roman gods. The very presence of such idols was considered pollution. Pilate had profaned the holy city. Pious Jews protested, but Pilate refused to budge, as any concession could be perceived as an insult to Caesar. Pilate also seized money from the Temple treasury in order to fund important public works. (Pilate's offenses against the Jews are detailed in Josephus, *Antiquities of the Jews* 18.3-4.)

Although the Temple officials raised protests at all the appropriate moments, they did not present a serious threat to Pilate or

> Both Pontius Pilate and Caiaphas were important men, respected and feared. Each man seems to have had a measure of respect for the other and his people — oddly mixed with a measure of contempt.

to Rome. History and Herod had schooled the priests in the art of compromise. They had the support of the aristocratic landholders and merchants. They knew how to protect the upper class's common interests through shrewd cooperation.

When Jesus foretold the Temple's destruction, He seemed threatening to Jerusalem's priests. Annas, Caiaphas, and their family probably saw themselves — with their diplomatic prudence and political savvy — as Jerusalem's only hope for survival.

Herod had removed and even massacred priests. What was to keep Rome from doing the same if the place began to appear unstable? And then what would happen to Jerusalem?

To the ears of the high-priestly family, the Apostles' language sounded subversive. It seemed to subvert not only the sacred order, but also the civic order, because the priests in Jerusalem were mediators not only between God and the Chosen People, but also between the Chosen People and their earthly rulers, the Romans.

To learn more about the lives and sacrifices of those first Christians given the task of spreading the gospel, read *Ministers and Martyrs: The Ultimate Catholic Guide to the Apostolic Age*.

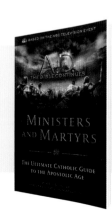

TERMS TO KNOW

- **Deacon:** An ordained minister of the Catholic Church. Ordained ministers include bishops (who are the successors of the Apostles), presbyters (priests, who assist the bishops), and deacons, who serve the Church in a number of ways.

- **Martyr:** Someone who is killed because of his religious beliefs.

- **Stoning:** Capital punishment for many crimes under Jewish law was carried out by stoning, unlike the crucifixion used by the Romans. Both punishments prolong death by torture.

BIBLICAL TOUCHSTONE

"Which of the prophets did your ancestors not persecute? They put to death those who foretold the coming of the righteous one, whose betrayers and murderers you have now become" (Acts 7:52).

Read Acts chapter 7, and focus in particular on the account of St. Stephen's martyrdom in Acts 7:54-60. Compare the events in Scripture with the story depicted in the episode. How do they differ in terms of:

- **St. Peter and St. Stephen's relationship**
- **The events that took place just before St. Stephen was martyred**
- **The words that were spoken by St. Stephen and others**
- **The other people present**
- **St. Stephen's last words**

SCRIPTURE AND THE SAINTS

Matthew 11:28-30

"Come to me, all you who labor and are burdened, and I will give you rest. Take my yoke upon you and learn from me, for I am meek and humble of heart; and you will find rest for your selves. For my yoke is easy, and my burden light."

Jesus offers His love to everyone in the world, and the Church is His instrument on Earth of salvation for all. Jesus invites the whole world into His love. In the same way, the Church offers Jesus' love to all.

The Apostles took on the burdens not only of the faithful and the newly converted, but of refugees of all backgrounds and faiths. As their tents filled, the Apostles became overwhelmed at the number who needed care. So the Twelve called the community together and explained that they would select seven wise and faithful men to serve the community while the Apostles focused on prayer and ministry. These seven men became the first ordained deacons of the Church.

 Did you know?

St. Stephen was among the first seven men to be ordained a deacon.

 Bl. Pope Paul VI

"God desires that the whole human race may become one People of God, form one Body of Christ, and be built up into one temple of the Holy Spirit."

 Acts 6:6

"They presented these men to the apostles who prayed and laid hands on them."

FOCUS QUESTION

The Apostles grew overwhelmed as their tents filled up with people just as Jesus had filled their nets with fish. Yet trusting in Jesus, they received all with love and mercy. It's no different for us. Blessed Mother Teresa asked, "You and I, we are the Church, no?" How can you be the Church?

DISCUSSION QUESTIONS

1. Leah tells Eva that if Boaz truly loved the people of Judea, he would give himself up. Do you agree? Is Boaz responsible for the deaths of innocent Judeans? If not, who is? Does it matter who is responsible?

2. What do you think Boaz's final thoughts were?

3. What are some ways St. Peter demonstrates his leadership in this episode?

4. Gamaliel counsels the Sanhedrin that they should "have nothing to do with [the Apostles], and let them go" (Acts 5:38). Does this warning remind you of another one received earlier by another character? Who?

5. St. Stephen — whose name means "crown" — was the first martyr of the Church. In what ways was his death similar to Jesus' death?

ANALYZING THE EPISODE

PHILIP: Forgive our intrusion. But these people are desperate. Can you help them? Even those who don't share the belief?

PETER: Jesus said, "Come to me, all you who labor and are burdened, and I will give you rest." And he meant all.

How do you think it felt for Peter and the Apostles to see the crowds of people timid and scared, all looking at them with pleading eyes? Two thousand years later, how does the Church continue to fulfill Christ's mission to help those who are weary and vulnerable?

GO FORTH AND EVANGELIZE

Blessed Mother Teresa said, "It is not enough for us to say: 'I love God,' but I also have to love my neighbor. How can you love God whom you do not see, if you do not love your neighbor whom you see, whom you touch, with whom you live?"

Sometimes it can be challenging to love our neighbors — those we don't get along with or those with different backgrounds, values, and beliefs. This week, resolve to do what the Apostles did: receive, care for, and love your neighbor, while never ceasing to speak the truth.

Make an effort to show love to people even when it's hard to do so. Forgive past wrongs, be kind and gentle to people you've quarreled with in the past. Welcome people who come from different places, or who have different beliefs or customs, or who struggle with different vices. Be a sign of Christ's unfailing love and mercy to them.

CLOSING PRAYER

"No one has greater love than this, to lay down one's life for one's friends" (John 15:13). This week, we ask the first martyr, St. Stephen, for his intercession. We pray to the Holy Trinity to help us embrace and speak the truth even amid trouble and persecution.

Prayer to St. Stephen the Protomartyr

Great St. Stephen, the scriptures tell us that your face was like an angel's as you witnessed to the truth of Christ.

Please ask the Most Holy Trinity to fill my soul and the souls of all my brothers and sisters throughout the world with a deep hunger for the truth that comes from the Heart of Jesus, and also with the loving courage to embrace and profess the truth even amid difficulties, confusion, and persecution.

May the serenity and peace which were yours at the hour of your stoning be ours as well as we wait in hope for the coming of the Lord Jesus, who lives and reigns forever and ever.

AMEN.

EPISODE 6
The Christians Are Scattered

37
Saul Begins Persecution of Christians

33
Christ Rises from the Dead

46
St. Paul's First Missionary Journey

64
Persecution of Christians Begins

71-80
Coliseum Built

IN THIS EPISODE

- St. Stephen is buried.
- Peter feels the pressure of looking after Jesus' flock.
- Caiaphas's position comes under threat from within his own family.
- Saul begins his persecution of the Church.

CITY OF JERUSALEM

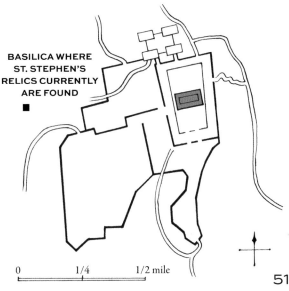

BASILICA WHERE ST. STEPHEN'S RELICS CURRENTLY ARE FOUND

0   1/4   1/2 mile

KEY CHARACTERS

St. Philip was one of the twelve Apostles, born in Galilee.

Saul was born to Jewish parents in Tarsus (in modern-day Turkey). Filled with anti-Christian zeal, he was present at the stoning of St. Stephen and went on to persecute the Church viciously.

Caiaphas is the Jewish high priest. His position comes under threat in this episode, even from members of his own family.

St. Peter is head of the Apostles. He feels some responsibility for the death of St. Stephen, but with the help of the Holy Spirit, he finds the strength to preach again.

THE CATHOLIC TAKEAWAY

Evil exists in the world because of our free will. God does not create evil, but He permits it because He respects our freedom and because — in one of His great mysteries — He can make good come from it.

The Apostles' Witness

BY MIKE AQUILINA

Jesus' execution solved nothing for his opponents. Quite the contrary. As reports went abroad of the Master's empty tomb, His popularity took an upturn.

The followers would be opposed, in turn, as their Master had been opposed. Opposition was an unavoidable part of the life of Jesus' disciples. Jesus had made it clear that such opposition would be universal, marked by Roman crucifixions and Jewish scourging (Mt. 23:34). And He assured His disciples that, contrary to all appearances, persecution would be the occasion of great blessings. "Blessed," He said, "are those who are persecuted for righteousness' sake" (Mt. 5:10).

Thus, persecution became, for the Church, a sign of success, a mark of resemblance to Jesus.

Two chapters of the Acts of the Apostles are dedicated to the story of Stephen, the first disciple to be persecuted unto death. Stephen's story provided Christians a framework for the understanding of all subsequent persecutions.

In every detail, Stephen's life and death are presented as a faithful imitation of the Passion of Jesus. Much later in the book, one of the Apostles would apply a term to Stephen that has become the Church's technical term for a Christian who is persecuted unto death. Stephen is called God's *martyros* (Acts 22:20). To Greek speakers of the first century, the word meant simply "witness" — a witness in a court of law. But the word came to have a special meaning for Christians and would soon be reserved for those who gave Christian testimony with their very lives.

The Church saw the death of the martyrs in sacrificial terms. In the book of Revelation, John saw "under the altar the souls of those who had been slain for the word of God and for the witness [*martyrian*] they had borne" (Rev. 6:9). The word he uses for altar means "place of sacrifice." The martyrs

> Martyrdom was indeed a vivid and compelling witness to the communion of life Christ shared with His disciples. "But if we have died with Christ," Paul said, "we believe that we shall also live with him" (Rom. 6:8).

are those who most perfectly carry out the exhortation of the Apostle Paul: "I appeal to you therefore, brethren, by the mercies of God, to present your bodies as a living sacrifice, holy and acceptable to God, which is your spiritual worship" (Rom. 12:1).

The early Christians looked at martyrdom as the most perfect imitation of the Eucharistic Christ. As Jesus laid down His life (John 15:13), He made an offering of His Body and Blood under the appearance of bread and wine (Luke 22:19-20). He identified Himself with those elements (John 6:51-56). So did the martyrs, in their turn. St. Paul foresaw that he would "be poured as a libation," a "sacrificial offering" (Phil. 2:17; see also 2 Tim. 4:6).

Martyrdom was indeed a vivid and compelling witness to the communion of life Christ shared with His disciples. "But if we have died with Christ," Paul said, "we believe that we shall also live with him" (Rom. 6:8). Christians could be God's children only if they were willing to share the suffering of the only-begotten Son — "we are . . . heirs with Christ, provided we suffer with him in order that we may also be glorified with him" (Rom. 8:16-17).

To learn more about the lives and sacrifices of those first Christians given the task of spreading the gospel, read *Ministers and Martyrs: The Ultimate Catholic Guide to the Apostolic Age.*

TERMS TO KNOW

- **"The desert and the parched land will be glad":** These words come from Isaiah 35 on the deliverance of Israel.

- **Rechitzah:** Part of the Jewish ritual of preparing a body for burial.

- **Purim:** Told in the book of Esther, the festival of Purim commemorates the salvation of the Jewish people in ancient Persia from Haman's plot "to destroy all the Jews in a single day" (Esther 3:5-7). Celebratory customs include donating to charity, exchanging gifts, a special meal, and dressing in costumes and masks.

BIBLICAL TOUCHSTONE

We read of Saul's persecution of the Church in Acts 8:1-3:

- "Now Saul was consenting to [St. Stephen's] execution."

- "On that day, there broke out a severe persecution of the church in Jerusalem, and all were scattered throughout the countryside of Judea and Samaria, except the apostles."

- "Devout men buried Stephen and made a loud lament over him."

- "Saul, meanwhile, was trying to destroy the church; entering house after house and dragging out men and women, he handed them over for imprisonment."

Why did Saul want to arrest the new Christians? What was his goal?

SCRIPTURE AND THE SAINTS

> **Genesis 50:20**
> "Even though you meant harm to me, God meant it for good, to achieve this present end, the survival of many people."

People were created with free will, and, since the Original Sin of Adam and Eve, people have often used their free will to do bad things. When bad things happen, it can be tempting to think that God has abandoned us. Or we might believe that our lives are made up of meaningless, random occurrences, and that our ultimate destinies depend on nothing more than the flip of a coin. But the existence of evil should not cause us to believe these falsehoods. God does not create evil, but He permits it because He respects our freedom.

The reality that the Lord allows people to do evil and hurt others is a mystery. But God can bring good even from the evil actions of His creatures. We can come closer to understanding this mystery through the example of Jesus Christ. From the greatest evil imaginable — the torture and murder of God the Son — has came the greatest good of our salvation. Christ suffered and died on the Cross in order to conquer evil and death. While we live, we can rely on our faith to understand this mystery; we will come to understand it truly in our eternal life with God.

 Did you know?
Before he was martyred, St. Thomas More said to his daughter, "Nothing can come but that which God wills. And I make me very sure that whatsoever that be, seem it never so bad in sight, it shall indeed be the best."

 St. Augustine
"For almighty God . . . because he is supremely good, would never allow any evil whatsoever to exist in his works if he were not so all-powerful and good as to cause good to emerge from evil itself."

FOCUS QUESTION

It's a great mystery that God can — and always does, even if we don't immediately see it — make good come from evil. Can you think of any way that God might make good come from the persecution of Christians?

DISCUSSION QUESTIONS

1. St. Peter and some of the Apostles partake in Jewish rituals, such as the rechitzah, or cleansing bath. Why would they do that?

2. What are some ways in which the Apostles might have been affected by the death of St. Stephen?

3. How would you describe St. Philip? What kind of person does he seem to be?

4. Why would Saul want to destroy the Church? Why does he want to terrorize the Apostles' followers?

5. It can be tempting to lose faith when confronted by evil in the world. How did the Apostles manage to keep their faith when they were being persecuted so fiercely? What can we learn from their example?

ANALYZING THE EPISODE

Much of the action between St. Peter and Saul in this episode is a dramatization, but Saul's persecution of the Church and the scattering of Christians were real. What will be the effect of the disciples' migration from Jerusalem? Reread Jesus' words to the disciples at His Ascension:

> "But you will receive power when the holy Spirit comes upon you, and you will be my witnesses in Jerusalem, throughout Judea and Samaria, and to the ends of the earth" (Acts 1:8).

How do Jesus' words foretell the progression of the events in later chapters in the Acts of the Apostles?

Does this understanding help us feel confident that Christ is in control of the spread of the gospel? Explain.

GO FORTH AND EVANGELIZE

In the Gospel of Matthew, Jesus tells us that worrying only makes an evil worse:

> "Do not worry about tomorrow; tomorrow will take care of itself. Sufficient for a day is its own evil" (Mt. 6:34).

This week, make a special effort not to worry and to be present to those around you so you can show them love. Here are some ideas — add your own to this list:

- Keeping in mind the redemptive value of suffering, offer up a trying time you will endure for the good of another.

- Read the Psalms, especially 9:9, 10; 46:1-3; 119:67, 71; and 147:3.

- With a friend who is going through trouble, offer this prayer: "Lord, grant me the strength to accept the things I cannot change, the courage to change the things I can, and the wisdom to know the difference."

- Spend time with your family and friends doing things they enjoy (and not necessarily the things you enjoy).

- _____
  _____
  _____

- _____
  _____
  _____

- _____
  _____
  _____
  _____

- _____
  _____
  _____

- Reach out to make new friends.

- _____
  _____
  _____

- "Cast all your worries upon [the Lord], because he cares for you" (1 Peter 5:7).

- _____
  _____
  _____

CLOSING PRAYER

Offer a Chaplet of Divine Mercy for all those who are persecuted in the world today.

Using rosary beads, begin with the Sign of the Cross. Then say one Our Father, one Hail Mary, and the Apostles' Creed.

On each Our Father bead say the following:

Eternal Father, I offer You the Body and Blood, Soul and Divinity of Your dearly beloved Son, our Lord Jesus Christ, in atonement for our sins and those of the whole world.

On each of the ten Hail Mary beads say the following:

For the sake of His sorrowful Passion, have mercy on us and on the whole world.

Conclude by saying three times:

Holy God, Holy Mighty One, Holy Immortal One, have mercy on us and on the whole world.

EPISODE 7

You Are All One in Christ Jesus

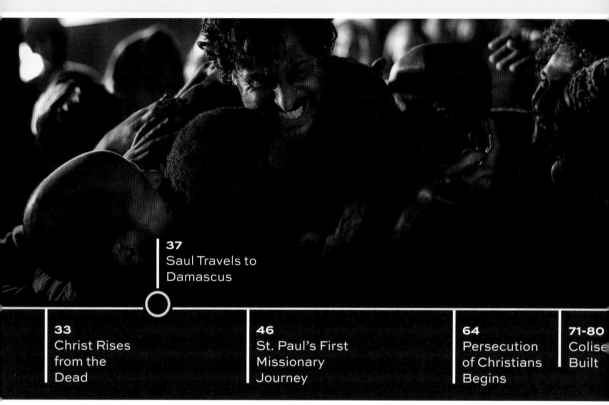

37
Saul Travels to
Damascus

33
Christ Rises
from the
Dead

46
St. Paul's First
Missionary
Journey

64
Persecution
of Christians
Begins

71-80
Colise
Built

IN THIS EPISODE

- St. Philip goes to Samaria. There he encounters Simon the Sorcerer, a local leader.

- Emperor Tiberius visits Jerusalem.

- St. Mary of Magdala encounters her old friend Joanna at Pilate's palace.

- Saul sets out for Damascus to search for Peter.

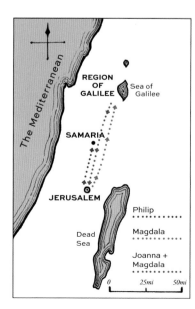

KEY CHARACTERS

 Joanna is the wife of Herod Antipas's house manager, Chuza. Joanna is one of the women who first witnessed the Resurrection (Luke 24:10).

 Simon the Sorcerer is a Samarian leader. He is a rival of St. Philip at first but soon is baptized a Christian.

 Tiberius Caesar is the Roman emperor. He ruled from A.D. 14 to 37. Historians believe he was murdered by Caligula's men or by Caligula himself.

 Caligula is the nephew of the emperor Tiberius. He went on to become emperor in A.D. 37 at age twenty-five.

 Caiaphas is the Jewish high priest. He tries to stop Saul's persecution of the Christians in Jerusalem.

 Saul was born to Jewish parents in Tarsus and is also a Roman citizen. In this episode, he continues his persecution of the remaining Christians.

 St. Philip is one of the twelve Apostles. He goes to Samaria, where he encounters Simon the Sorcerer.

 Pontius Pilate is the prefect of the Roman province of Judea. Eager to leave Jerusalem, he lobbies Tiberius for a promotion that would send him to Syria.

 ## THE CATHOLIC TAKEAWAY

The Divine is good, beautiful, and true. Wisdom, one of the gifts of the Holy Spirit, helps us to discern true from false, good from bad, and beautiful from distorted.

The Conversion of Saul

BY MIKE AQUILINA

Among the Church's persecutors, Saul was singular in his zeal, unabashed in his purpose. He went about "breathing threats and murder against the disciples of the Lord" (Acts 9:1). Ravaging the Church, and "entering house after house, he dragged off men and women and committed them to prison" (Acts 8:3). The mere mention of Saul's name was enough to strike fear in the heart of those who followed Jesus' way (see Acts 9:13-14).

From his earliest days, Saul had sense of divine calling. His birthplace, Tarsus, was a bustling coastal city and administrative center for the Roman province of Cilicia (what is now southeastern Turkey). Like his father, Saul was a tradesman — a tentmaker. Like his father, he held Roman citizenship, a coveted privilege. Like his father, he observed the doctrine and discipline of the Pharisees.

A prodigy, he went early to Jerusalem to study in the great center of Jewish learning, where he studied under the renowned rabbi Gamaliel. He also fell under the influence of radical ideas. Some teachers believed that faithful observance of the Torah was the pre-condition of God's saving action — and that sectarians like Jesus were discouraging people from keeping the Law. Jesus, after all, had repeatedly violated the laws regarding the Sabbath — healing people, encouraging His disciples to pick grain, and so on. He had even declared Himself to be "Lord of the Sabbath" (Mt. 12:8). thus putting Himself in the place of God.

Saul believed that Jesus' disciples should be given a choice. They should adopt a strict observance of the Law — or they should die, so that they would not bring divine judgment down on the rest of the nation.

The disciples fled Jerusalem, but they were not cowed into silence. St. Luke reports that "those who were scattered went about preaching the word" (Acts 8:4). This new persecution, like the death of Jesus before it, just exacerbated the problem for the Jerusalem authorities. Wherever the disciples fled, they made new disciples.

> Accepting the Messiah was not something alien to Paul's Jewishness. Indeed, for all the time he was a Pharisee, it was what he had been waiting for.

The growth of the Church surely fueled Saul's fury. He believed he was on a divine mission — "as to zeal a persecutor of the church, as to righteousness under the law blameless" (Phil. 3:6). As he traveled to bring the persecution to Syria, however, something happened.

Struck to the ground, he received a revelation from God. And he learned that Jesus was the Messiah he had sought. He ceased to be a persecutor of Jesus and began to be a disciple. He converted, but he did not abandon the religion of Israel. Long after his incident on the road to Damascus, he made it clear that he was still a Jew (Acts 21:39) and still a Pharisee (Acts 23:6). The people of Israel would always be, for him, "my brethren, my kinsmen by race" (Rom. 9:3). Accepting the Messiah was not something alien to his Jewishness. Indeed, for all the time he was a Pharisee, it was what he had been waiting for.

To learn more about the lives and sacrifices of those first Christians given the task of spreading the gospel, read *Ministers and Martyrs: The Ultimate Catholic Guide to the Apostolic Age.*

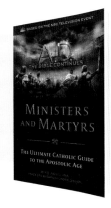

TERMS TO KNOW

- **Roman Empire:** Rome had been governed as a republic for more than five hundred years when Julius Caesar seized power as a dictator. Following his assassination in 44 B.C., Rome was ruled by triumvirates until Augustus was made the first emperor twenty-seven years before the birth of Christ. In contrast with the Jews, whose beliefs, rituals, and traditions were based on worship of a single God, the Romans were pagans who worshiped several deities.

- **Roman emperor:** The absolute ruler of the Roman Empire, which at the time of Christ encompassed almost all of Europe, Turkey, Syria, Israel, and part of North Africa. The Roman emperor had power over the military and the citizens. In ancient times, the Roman emperor was probably the most powerful person on Earth.

BIBLICAL TOUCHSTONE

Trace the events that take place in chapter 8 of Acts. Simon the Sorcerer received the sacrament of Baptism, making him a Christian. However, he soon reverted to his old ways as a charlatan because he lacked the discernment and wisdom to know what was true and good from what was false and harmful. Reflect on Acts 8:9-25, keeping in mind the following:

- **Like the Apostles at Pentecost, Christians must receive the Holy Spirit. As Catholics, we receive an outpouring of the Holy Spirit with the sacrament of Confirmation. What does Acts 8:9-25 teach us about the necessity of Baptism and of Confirmation, which perfects baptismal grace?**

- **How does this part of the Bible show us the availability of Christ's mercy to all sinners: men, women; the simple, the clever; the poor, the rich; the upright, the corrupt; and so forth?**

- **Christian tradition calls Simon the Sorcerer the father of heretics and the founder of Gnosticism. Why do you think this is so?**

SCRIPTURE AND THE SAINTS

Wisdom, one of the gifts of the Holy Spirit, is a virtue because wisdom attracts us to those things that are true and good. When we encounter those things that are true and beautiful, we are better prepared to encounter the invisible realities they represent. "Steeped in wisdom, man passes through visible realities to those which are unseen" (*Gaudium et Spes* 15). The gift of wisdom is necessary in this life with all its temptations that appeal to our selfishness and pride. But when we know the truth, we are set free in Christ — just like the Samaritans freed by St. Philip in the name of Jesus: "For unclean spirits, crying out in a loud voice, came out of many possessed people, and many paralyzed and crippled people were cured" (Acts 8:7).

 Did you know?

Jesus' associations with women, including St. Mary of Magdala, Joanna, and others, were highly unusual. First-century Palestinian Judaism cautioned against speaking with women in public.

 Colossians 2:8

"See to it that no one captivate you with an empty, seductive philosophy according to human tradition, according to the elemental powers of the world and not according to Christ."

 Pope St. Gregory

"There are in truth three states of the converted: the beginning, the middle, and the perfection. In the beginning, they experience the charms of sweetness; in the middle, the contests of temptation; and in the end, the fullness of perfection."

FOCUS QUESTION

Jesus separates the sheep from the goats. We have many opportunities every day to exercise the wisdom to know what is good and what is bad and to act accordingly. What are your biggest challenges when it comes to discerning the truth? Ask the Holy Spirit to help you be wise and open to receiving God's will.

DISCUSSION QUESTIONS

1. St. Philip meets Simon the Sorcerer. How does the power given to the Apostles by Jesus differ from magic?

2. As St. Philip heals the Samaritan woman, he says to her, "I release you from your prison." How does Jesus free all humanity from a kind of imprisonment?

3. Trumpets blast, and all the Romans kneel in the presence of the Roman emperor. How is the respect we show our political leaders different? Why?

4. Saul claims to be doing God's will. Is he? Explain.

5. In this episode, what contrasts do we see between misguided leaders and true ones?

ANALYZING THE EPISODE

St. Peter celebrates Holy Mass with the disciples. Each Holy Mass stretching back to the Last Supper commemorates Jesus' Sacrifice on the Cross through the Holy Eucharist. The Mass is an unbloody re-presentation (that makes present) His sacrifice. Each day, Catholics in every country gather to be made present in Christ's Sacrifice, which takes away the sins of the world.

PETER: Jesus told us that this bread and wine were His Body and Blood.

Read the Bread of Life Discourse in John 6:21-63.

For a free video on this part of the Bible and the Eucharist's connection to the Cross and Holy Mass, visit **SophiaSketchPad.org.**

GO FORTH AND EVANGELIZE

In Jesus Christ we are given God's love fully revealed. He is the truth, and His love enlightens the world. We are created in God's image, and we are called to live in the truth.

Make a special effort this week to ensure that everything you do, say, and surround yourself with reflects the truth, beauty, and goodness of the Lord.

- Read the Ten Commandments, and in particular the Eighth Commandment. Discuss with your family how it requires Christians not only to refrain from lying, but actively to bear witness to the truth.

- Be mindful of the movies and television shows that you and your children watch.

- Cancel any print or digital content subscriptions that corrupt your home.

- Make sure everything in your home is either useful or beautiful (or both!).

- Don't use foul language or gossip. Apply the golden rule in everyday life when discerning whether to reveal the truth to someone who asks for it.

- Bring pieces of sacred art into your home. "Sacred art is true and beautiful when its form corresponds to its particular vocation: evoking and glorifying, in faith and adoration, the transcendent mystery of God" (*Catechism of the Catholic Church* 2502)

- Meditate on Ephesians 4:25: "Therefore, putting away falsehood, speak the truth, each one to his neighbor, for we are members one of another."

CLOSING PRAYER

Jesus tells us in the Gospel of John, "And you will know the truth, and the truth will set you free" (John 8:32). In this episode, St. Mary of Magdala and Joanna say the Lord's Prayer together. This week, let us pray the words our Savior gave us. We ask Him to set us free in His truth and to help us discern the truth of His will, which is always good, true, and beautiful.

Our Father, who art in Heaven,

Hallowed be Thy Name.

Thy Kingdom come;

Thy will be done on Earth as it is in Heaven.

Give us this day our daily bread,

and forgive us our trespasses as we forgive those who trespass against us.

And lead us not into temptation,

But deliver us from evil.

AMEN.

EPISODE 8
On the Way to Damascus

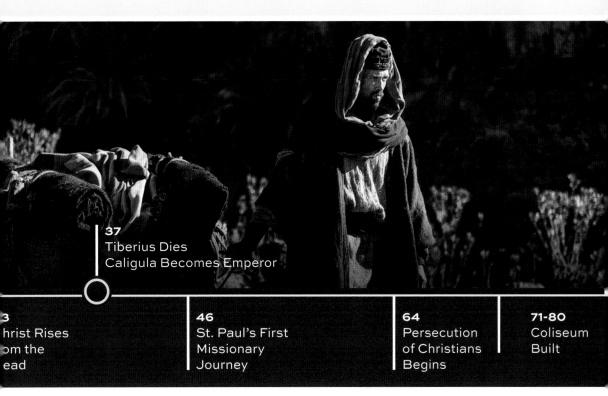

37
Tiberius Dies
Caligula Becomes Emperor

3
hrist Rises
ɔm the
ead

46
St. Paul's First
Missionary
Journey

64
Persecution
of Christians
Begins

71-80
Coliseum
Built

IN THIS EPISODE

- Saul encounters the risen Jesus on the road to Damascus. He is blinded and converts.

- Peter and John join Philip in Samaria to lay hands on the new converts so they may receive the Holy Spirit.

- Simon the Sorcerer misguidedly tries to buy the Holy Spirit from Sts. Peter and John.

- Jerusalem learns that Tiberius is dead and Caligula is the new emperor.

- Jesus sends Ananias to heal Saul and instruct him to bring the gospel to the Gentiles.

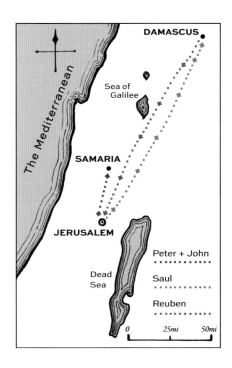

KEY CHARACTERS

 Jesus Christ is God the Son, who became man to be with us. He died for our sins and rose again on the third day in accordance with the Scriptures. He ascended into heaven and is seated at the right hand of the Father.

 Ananias is a disciple of Christ in Damascus. Jesus tells him to seek out Saul and instruct him to bring His message to the Gentiles.

 Chuza is the house manager of Herod Antipas and the husband of Joanna. (See Luke 8:3.)

 "Claudia" is the wife of Pontius Pilate. She bonds with the emperor Tiberius while he is staying in their palace but is troubled by disturbing dreams that he is murdered.

 St. Peter is head of the Apostles. He and St. John join St. Philip in Samaria so the new converts may receive the Holy Spirit. He sends Simon the Sorcerer away when Simon tries to buy the Holy Spirit from him.

 Pontius Pilate is the prefect of the Roman province of Judea. He loses hope of a promotion and move to Syria when he learns the emperor has died.

 Saul was born to Jewish parents in Tarsus. He viciously persecutes the Church and sets off for Damascus in pursuit of St. Peter. On the way there, he has a life-changing experience.

THE CATHOLIC TAKEAWAY

If you repent and ask for God's mercy, He will always give it to you. God can use all of humanity, even the most unlikely of us, for the good of His Holy Church.

The Breaking of the Bread

BY MIKE AQUILINA

Communion is the condition of fellowship shared by those who have a covenant relationship with one another. In Hebrew the word for this bond is *chaburah*. In Greek it is *koinonia*.

Communion is a kind of friendship, but it is more than that. It is more like a family bond; and both Hebrew and Greek usage in the time of the Apostles suggested a religious dimension to the bond. The word *chaburah* described a group of friends who gathered for religious discussion and common prayer. They met weekly on the eve of the Sabbath (and the eves of holy days) for a formal meal.

A communion is something more than a community. It is closer-knit, gathered for the most important purpose on Earth as well as the most festive. It is defined by a common meal and sacred conversation. For the Jews of Jesus' time, such a meal renewed their most basic identity — as Israel, as God's Chosen People.

Although the Jews shared a covenant with God, they dared not go the extra step and call it a communion. Yet, for Christians, God's Incarnation changed the terms of the divine-human relationship. God had made a New Covenant in the blood of Christ, and He had done so at a chaburah meal (Luke 22:20). At that meal, Jesus — God incarnate — declared His disciples to be no longer slaves but friends (John 15:15). He sanctified them through His blood (Heb. 13:12). The shared blood of Jesus made it possible for His disciples to "enter the sanctuary" and enjoy communion with God (Heb. 10:19). Through the Incarnation, Jesus made it possible for His disciples to enjoy a share of His own eternal sonship, by sharing in His Flesh and Blood (Heb. 2:14). The language of sharing, so often used by the Apostles, is the language of communion — the verb form of the noun *koinonia*.

The Acts of the Apostles presents the Church as such a communion: "And they

> A communion is something more than a community. It is closer-knit, gathered for the most important purpose on Earth as well as the most festive. It is defined by a common meal and sacred conversation.

devoted themselves to the apostles' teaching and fellowship [*koinonia*], to the breaking of bread and the prayers" (Acts 2:42).

The "breaking of bread" was ever afterward the sign of the Church's fellowship and of communion with God. God had drawn His people collectively into fellowship with Him. They could not sustain that relationship with Him unless they kept communion with one another.

Fellowship did not depend on race, ethnicity, or past history. Even the most notorious enemies of Christ were welcome to communion, if they repented. After his conversion, Saul was delighted to share "the right hand of fellowship [*koinonias*]" with the inner circle of Jesus' original disciples: Peter, James, and John (see Gal. 2:9).

The sign of the Church's deep fellowship was "the breaking of the bread" (see Acts 2:42, 46; 20:7; see also Luke 24:35). The disciples of Jesus shared among themselves the common ritual meal their Master had established. As in friendship or family, the meal was a sign of the bond, and the shared meal strengthened the bond.

To learn more about the lives and sacrifices of those first Christians given the task of spreading the gospel, read *Ministers and Martyrs: The Ultimate Catholic Guide to the Apostolic Age.*

TERMS TO KNOW

- **The Way:** A phrase used by the early Christian community to describe itself. Jesus said, "I am the way and the truth and the life" (John 14:6).

- **Succession:** Although they were absolute rulers, Roman emperors did not claim the title of king. Upon the death of one emperor, power was often passed through the family, but sometimes by conquest or murder.

- **Visions:** Throughout the Old and New Testaments, God used dreams and visions to speak to people, including Abraham, Jacob, Joseph, Sts. Peter, Paul, and John, and many others. The visions experienced in this episode by Saul and Ananais are likewise based on the Bible. The visions experienced by the character of Claudia are a mixture of truth and fiction. The only mention of Pilate's wife in Scripture comes from the Gospel of Matthew: "While [Pilate] was still seated on the bench, his wife sent him a message, 'Have nothing to do with that righteous man. I suffered much in a dream today because of him'" (Mt. 27:19).

BIBLICAL TOUCHSTONE

Read Acts chapter 9, and reflect on the conversion of St. Paul:

- **Jesus says to Saul, "I am Jesus, whom you are persecuting." But Saul has been persecuting Jesus' followers. Why does Jesus say that Saul has been persecuting Him?**

- **Saul was blinded. How many days went by before he could see again? Is there any significance to that number?**

- **What connections can you make between Saul's encounter with Jesus and Proverbs 3:6: "In all your ways be mindful of him, and he will make straight your paths"?**

- **How can this event give us hope in the Lord's unfailing mercy?**

SCRIPTURE AND THE SAINTS

Matthew 5:44
"But I say to you, love your enemies, and pray for those who persecute you."

In his time, there might have been no greater enemy of Christianity than Saul, and yet God used him as an instrument of love, putting all his passion and zeal to good use. Jesus tells Ananias in a vision that Saul is "a chosen instrument of mine." Despite all of Saul's vicious anger and violence against the Christians, even despite his participation in the stoning of St. Stephen, God chose him "to carry my name before Gentiles, kings, and Israelites" (Acts 9:15).

Our faith allows us to know for certain that God will always make good come from evil, even if we don't see or understand it immediately. For this reason and for many others, we should pray for our enemies as Jesus commands.

 Did you know?
Saul is often depicted in paintings as falling off his horse upon encountering Jesus on the road to Damascus. It is indeed likely he would have been on horseback. Scripture, however, says only that he "fell to the ground" (Acts 9:4).

 St. Thomas Aquinas
"If, then, you are looking for the way by which you should go, take Christ, because He Himself is the way."

 St. John Chrysostom
"Let no one mourn that he has fallen again and again; for forgiveness has risen from the grave."

FOCUS QUESTION

The people Jesus chose to carry out His mission seem to have many flaws. Peter denied Jesus three times. The Apostles fell asleep when they were supposed to be keeping watch. Saul raged vicious persecution against the Church. Is there anyone the Lord cannot use as an instrument of His good?

DISCUSSION QUESTIONS

1. Saul set out for Damascus looking for people "who belonged to the way" (Acts 9:2). What are some instances of the use of the word *way* in this episode? How do they relate to Jesus?

2. What are some reasons Jesus might have sent Ananias to restore Saul's sight rather than doing it Himself?

3. Sts. Peter and John go to Damascus to lay hands on the newly baptized Christians, that they may receive an outpouring of the Holy Spirit. Ananias lays hands on Saul so that Jesus may restore his health. What can we learn from these examples about sacramental life in the Church?

4. For what reasons did early Church writers consider Simon the Sorcerer the first heretic?

5. Jesus calls us to love not only God and our neighbor but even our enemies. He also tells us that in order to receive forgiveness ourselves, we must forgive those who hurt us. What can we learn from the conversion of Saul that we might remember when we struggle to love our enemies?

ANALYZING THE EPISODE

He fell to the ground and heard a voice.

JESUS: Saul, Saul, why are you persecuting me?

SAUL: Who are you, sir?

JESUS: I am Jesus, whom you are persecuting.

What do you think was going though Saul's mind when he heard these words? What might be some reasons he was struck blind?

Jesus equates Himself with the Church. Why is this important?

GO FORTH AND EVANGELIZE

Jesus' mercy was deep enough to use even someone like Saul for the good of His Church. Indeed, there is no sin you can commit that God would not forgive if you are sorry, resolve not commit it again, and ask for forgiveness.

This week, be a shining example of God's mercy by being merciful yourself.

Forgive those who trespass against you. In Matthew's Gospel, Peter asks Jesus how often he must forgive his brother: "'How often must I forgive him? As many as seven times?' Jesus answered, 'I say to you, not seven times but seventy-seven times'" (Mt. 18:21-22).

- In a short journal entry, reflect on this passage from the *Catechism of the Catholic Church*: "He who lives by God's merciful love is ready to respond to the Lord's call: 'Go; first be reconciled to your brother'" (*Catechism of the Catholic Church* 1424).

- Make a special effort to be reconciled to those who have hurt you.

- Are you currently holding a grudge? Is there someone you could contact to express forgiveness for a past wrong?

- Is there someone you need to ask forgiveness from?

- If you know someone who is struggling with guilt or with how to avoid sin, suggest that he or she talk to a priest in Confession.

- If someone you know is thinking about going to Confession, encourage him or her.

- Learn more about the Corporal and Spiritual Works of Mercy and practice them often.

- For one month, try extra hard to be slow to anger and to forgive wrongs.

CLOSING PRAYER

This week, let us pray that God will use us as He did Saul of Tarsus: as instruments of His peace, love, and mercy.

PEACE PRAYER ATTRIBUTED TO ST. FRANCIS OF ASSISI

Lord, make me an instrument of Your
peace. Where there is hatred, let me
sow love; where there is injury, pardon;
where there is doubt, faith; where there
is despair, hope; where there is darkness,
light; where there is sadness, joy.

O Divine Master, grant that I may not so
much seek to be consoled as to console;
to be understood as to understand; to
be loved as to love. For it is in giving
that we receive; it is in pardoning that
we are pardoned; it is in dying that we
are born again to eternal life.

EPISODE 9
Caligula's Statue

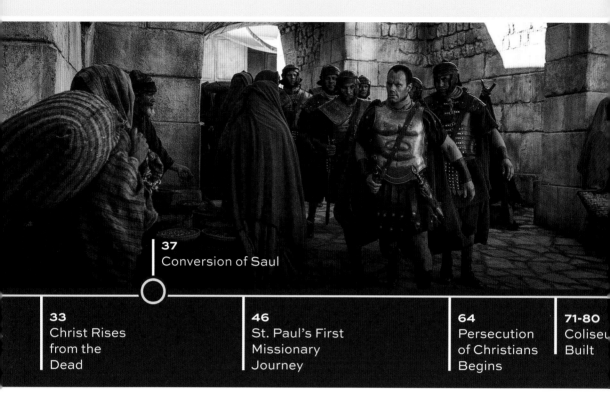

37
Conversion of Saul

33
Christ Rises
from the
Dead

46
St. Paul's First
Missionary
Journey

64
Persecution
of Christians
Begins

71-80
Coliseu
Built

IN THIS EPISODE

- Saul arrives back in Jerusalem, where he meets with Peter and the disciples.

- The disciples agree to welcome Saul into the Church.

- Caligula orders a statue of himself to be placed inside the Temple.

- Saul is captured and imprisoned by Reuben.

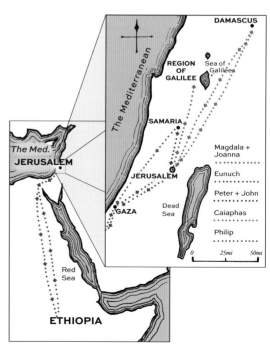

KEY CHARACTERS

 Herod Antipas is the tetrarch of Galilee (a tetrarch was a ruler of a principality). He sees a political opportunity in the controversy surrounding Caligula's statue.

 St. Barnabas is a disciple of Christ. He helps bring Saul from Damascus back to Jerusalem and vouches for him to St. Peter.

 Caligula is the new Roman emperor. He orders that a statue of himself be placed in the Temple — a command that sends Jerusalem into turmoil.

 Saul is a new convert to Christianity. St. Peter and many of the disciples are at first wary of welcoming him into the Church because he had so recently persecuted the Christians.

 St. Peter is head of the Church. After St. Barnabas vouches for Saul, he agrees to welcome Saul into the Church.

 ## THE CATHOLIC TAKEAWAY

All people are created in the image of God with equal dignity. We are all members of the same Body.

Faith Comes to the Gentiles

BY MIKE AQUILINA

The relationship between Romans and Jews was uneasy at best, mutually antagonistic at worst. There is ample evidence in the New Testament of the Jews' horror of Gentiles in general and Romans in particular. Even Jesus said that an obstinate sinner should be treated "as a Gentile and a tax collector" (Mt. 18:17). The chief priests, for their part, worried that Jesus' popularity would begin to look like a rebellion — and would bring about a crackdown from the occupying powers: "If we let him go on thus, every one will believe in him, and the Romans will come and destroy both our holy place and our nation" (John 11:48).

Yet the Gospel also sounded a new and hopeful note for the Romans. Both Matthew and Luke relate the story of a Roman centurion who sought healing for his beloved servant. The elders of his town begged Jesus on the centurion's behalf, perhaps assuming that the Master would not listen to a Gentile. "He is worthy to have you do this for him," they said, "for he loves our nation, and he built us our synagogue" (Luke 7:4-5). Eventually the man pleaded his own case, moving Jesus to exclaim: "Truly, I say to you, not even in Israel have I found such faith" (Mt. 8:10).

The story is significant, because it shows that a Gentile — even a Roman and even a high-ranking military officer — could have the kind of faith that God sought from Israel.

Nor is the story unique. Another centurion, seeing Jesus crucified, was moved to confess the Master's divinity: "Truly this man was the Son of God!" (Mark 15:39).

> This story is significant because it shows that a Gentile — even a Roman, and even a high-ranking military officer — could have the kind of faith that God sought from Israel.

In the Acts of the Apostles, St. Luke presents a Roman centurion who was also a believer in the God of Israel, a man who "gave alms liberally to the people, and prayed constantly to God" (Acts 10:2). Cornelius received an extraordinary revelation from God regarding Peter, whom he sent soldiers to summon from Joppa. By the end of the incident, God had made clear to Peter that Israel's dietary taboos were no longer to be observed (Acts 10:45).

These developments led to conflict. Jewish Christians of a traditionalist bent

opposed what they saw as an abrogation of the ancient law (Acts 11:2-18). They vehemently protested Peter's sitting down to eat with Romans. The controversy continued as Paul and Barnabas made more converts among the Gentiles. It was settled only when the Apostles met in council (Acts 15) and concluded that they "should not trouble those of the Gentiles who turn to God" (Acts 15:19).

Rome, the great Gentile capital, in fact would become the great Christian capital on Earth. The trajectory of Luke's narrative is Romeward. Paul was inexorably drawn there — in spite of many obstacles — "resolved in the Spirit." He considered Macedonia, Achaia, and Jerusalem to be steps along the way: "After I have been there, I must also see Rome" (Acts 19:21). The Lord Himself made clear to Paul that the imperial capital should be his destination.

Peter, too, made his way there (1 Peter 5:13); and Christians would eventually cast the two Apostles as the new founders of the city.

To learn more about the lives and sacrifices of those first Christians given the task of spreading the gospel, read *Ministers and Martyrs: The Ultimate Catholic Guide to the Apostolic Age.*

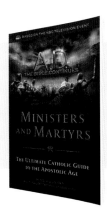

TERMS TO KNOW

- **St. Paul:** After his conversion, Saul of Tarsus became known as Paul. Many assume that the Lord changed his name, as He did Peter's (Mt. 16:18; John 1:41-42). But Saul's name did not actually change. Saul was both a Jew and a Roman citizen. He was given the Hebrew name Saul by his parents, and his Greek name was Paul (Acts 16:37; 22:25-28). When Saul became a Christian and set out to bring the gospel to the Gentiles, he began using his Greek name, which would have been more familiar to them.

BIBLICAL TOUCHSTONE

The period after Saul ended his persecution of the Church is known as "the Church at Peace." Read and mediate on the following verse from Acts.

- **Acts 9:31**
  "The Church throughout all Judea, Galilee, and Samaria was at peace. It was being built up and walked in the fear of the Lord, and with the consolation of the holy Spirit it grew in numbers."

- **How do you think it felt for the Apostles and the disciples to realize their persecution from Saul had ended?**

- **This passage is significant because it describes Christians in terms not only of individual believers, but as organized religious communities. Why is that important?**

SCRIPTURE AND THE SAINTS

Galatians 3:26-28

"For through faith you are all children of God in Christ Jesus. For all of you who were baptized into Christ have clothed yourselves with Christ. There is neither Jew nor Greek, there is neither slave nor free person, there is not male and female; for you are all one in Christ Jesus."

All are equal in the sight of God. Although people differ in terms of their sex, age, talents, physical strength, interests, and other traits, their equality "rests essentially on their dignity as persons and the rights that flow from it" (*Catechism of the Catholic Church* 1935). But the fact that we are all created equal by God does not mean we are all the same. Within that universal call to holiness, we each have an individual vocation to discern.

 Did you know?

St. Paul wrote about his visit to Jerusalem in his epistle to the Galatians. "I was unknown personally to the churches of Judea that are in Christ; they only kept hearing that 'the one who once was persecuting us is now preaching the faith he once tried to destroy'" (Gal. 1:22-23).

St. Thérèse of Lisieux

"The value of life does not depend upon the place we occupy. It depends upon the way we occupy that place."

Wisdom 6:7

"For the Ruler of all shows no partiality, nor does he fear greatness, / Because he himself made the great as well as the small, and provides for all alike."

FOCUS QUESTION

We are all members of one family and are all individual members of the Body of Christ. Did Jesus treat repentant people differently based on their talents, or their sex, or their income, et cetera? What signs of Jesus' mercy do we see in this episode?

DISCUSSION QUESTIONS

1. After he was baptized, Saul immediately began preaching in the synagogues. Why is this especially upsetting to the Jews in Damascus?

2. The personal qualities that made Saul such a threat to the Apostles — fanaticism, zeal, and obsession — are now being put to good use by God in the form of faith, enthusiasm, and devotion. Have you ever experienced or witnessed a similar conversion of vices to virtues?

3. Why are Caiaphas and Antipas so upset about Caligula's plans for a statue of himself to be erected in the Temple?

4. How would you react if the president or a member of Congress demanded that a statue of himself be put up in your church? Why?

5. St. Mary of Magdala and Joanna are not among the twelve Apostles, yet they were very important to Jesus and were among the first witnesses to the Resurrection. How do they work to sustain the Church?

ANALYZING THE EPISODE

- **Acts 10:34-35**
  "Then Peter proceeded to speak and said, 'In truth, I see that God shows no partiality. Rather, in every nation whoever fears him and acts uprightly is acceptable to him.'"

St. Mary of Magdala and Joanna were both healed by Jesus on the same day (Luke 8:3). Although one was rich and the other poor, Jesus treated them both as equals. We are all created in the image of God with equal dignity. Jesus never refuses His mercy to those who ask for it in earnest. What signs of this truth do we see in this episode?

GO FORTH AND EVANGELIZE

This week, focus your evangelization efforts on building up the Church by building up the individual parts of Christ's Body.

- Establish common interests with newcomers to your neighborhood and your parish.

- Organize informal get-togethers or potluck dinners around special feast days.

- If a family member or a friend is a lapsed Catholic, warmly invite him or her to take a step back toward the Church. Perhaps invite the person to attend Mass with you or even just to pray with you.

- Offer to drive family and friends to Confession.

- Learn more about the Catholic teaching of solidarity by reading a book about it or discussing it with a priest.

CLOSING PRAYER

Pope John Paul II in his 1988 encyclical *Dignitatum Mulieris* affirmed St. Mary of Magdala as "Apostle to the Apostles." This week, we pray for her intercession to ask God to help us know and act on the truth that we are all members of the same Body of Christ.

St. Mary of Magdala, woman of faith,
pray for those whose belief is tested —
who feel that they are not good enough
— who feel they do not belong.
Guide us all through your story
to the hope of resurrection.
Our Father . . .
Hail Mary . . .
Glory be . . .

EPISODE 10
Saul of Tarsus

39
Saul Returns to Jerusalem

33
Christ Rises
from the
Dead

46
St. Paul's First
Missionary
Journey

64
Persecution
of Christians
Begins

71-80
Colise
Built

IN THIS EPISODE

- James the Just arrives in Jerusalem and strikes a truce with Caiaphas on behalf of the Church.

- The disciples send Saul away to Tarsus for his own safety.

- Tabitha is beaten and Joanna imprisoned.

- Gabra meets with Levi to discuss a zealot uprising.

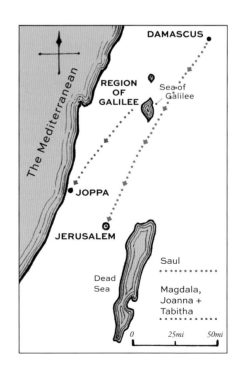

KEY CHARACTERS

 Jesus Christ is God the Son. In this episode, He appears to St. James and reignites his faith.

 James the Just was the first bishop of Jerusalem according to tradition. The epistle of James in the New Testament is attributed to him.

 "Leah" is the wife of Caiaphas, the Jewish high priest. She is furious with her husband for not taking a harder stance against the Christians.

 Pontius Pilate is the governor of the Roman province of Judea. He refuses to tolerate Christians in his palace and brutally beats Tabitha and imprisons Joanna. The historical Pilate had been removed from office by A.D. 36, about five years before Saul returned to Tarsus.

 Saul is a recent convert to Christianity. His bold preaching causes trouble for him and the disciples in Jerusalem, and the disciples send him to Tarsus.

 St. Simon is one of the twelve Apostles. He is called Simon the Zealot because of his strict adherence to Jewish and Canaanite law.

THE CATHOLIC TAKEAWAY

God, in His divine providence, gives us chances to cooperate with His plans.

Divisions in the Church

BY MIKE AQUILINA

It did not take long for serious divisions to threaten the unity of the Church. St. Paul lamented the "divisions" in the Church in Corinth (1 Cor. 11:18) — and he feared that legitimate differences were producing illegitimate factions. To depart, in any way, from the apostolic teaching about Jesus Christ was to preach or worship a different Christ. It was a form of idolatry, and so it was the most loathsome of sins.

Heresy — the word is now a technical term that denotes the denial of revealed truth, the adherence to a religious opinion that contradicts Christian dogma. St. Peter warned against it in the New Testament (2 Peter 2:1).

The apostolic age saw many threats to Christian unity. They were not alternative forms of Christianity, equally as valid as the Apostles' preaching. They were counterfeits, as worthless, false, and destructive as phony currency. Most of the heresies that would arise in later centuries were simply variations on themes that had already been evident in the apostolic age. A few examples follow.

Simony is the idea that spiritual goods can be bought or sold. It is named for Simon of Samaria, a strange figure in the Acts of the Apostles (Acts 8:9-24). A magician, he made great claims for himself. Hearing the Gospel, however, he accepted Christ and was baptized; but, seeing the Apostles' evident power, he was filled with envy, and offered them money if they would share their power with him. Peter cursed Simon for his blasphemous proposal, and Simon was subdued by fear. But there is some evidence that Simon persisted in false teaching and eventually established himself as a teacher in Rome.

Judaizing: in his letter to the Galatians, St. Paul refuted the idea that Gentiles must first submit to Jewish law before they could be admitted to the Church. Judaizers in Galatia were requiring Gentile converts to undergo circumcision and keep a kosher diet. Paul insisted that these ritual laws had been rendered obsolete by the sacrifice

> The apostolic age saw many threats to Christian unity. They were not alternative forms of Christianity, equally as valid as the Apostles' preaching. They were counterfeits, as worthless, false, and destructive as phony currency.

of Jesus Christ. The Apostles meeting in council also condemned the practices of the Judaizers (Acts 15). The problem would continue to resurface throughout the early centuries of the Church, but the movements always remained small.

Docetism: the name was coined later to describe a heresy already evident in the time of the Apostles. It describes those who denied Jesus' true humanity, teaching instead that He only seemed to be a man. (The Greek word for "to seem" is *dokeo*.) The letters of St. John deal repeatedly with the problem and prescribe excommunication as its solution (2 John 1:7-11; see also 1 John 4:2-3).

Gnosticism is the name given by later Fathers to the elitist heresies that emphasized esoteric "knowledge" (Greek *gnosis*) over faith and love. St. Paul may have been combating these ideas when he warned the Corinthians: "Knowledge puffs up, but love builds up. If any one imagines that he knows something, he does not yet know as he ought to know. But if one loves God, one is known by him" (1 Cor. 8:1-3).

To learn more about the lives and sacrifices of those first Christians given the task of spreading the gospel, read *Ministers and Martyrs: The Ultimate Catholic Guide to the Apostolic Age.*

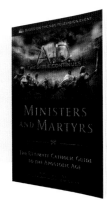

TERMS TO KNOW

- **Chariot:** An open carriage drawn by animals, usually horses. It was used in many places in the ancient world for travel, processions, and games.

- **Eunuch:** A slave or servant who had been castrated so as to pose little threat to the ruler he served. Eunuchs were forbidden to enter the Temple in Jerusalem (Deut. 23:1).

- **Providence:** This term describes God's wisdom in ordering all the events in the world so that humanity can share in His eternal truth, beauty, and goodness.

- **Yom Kippur:** The Jewish day of atonement and the holiest day of the year for the Jewish people. Yom Kippur is marked by fasting, repentance, prayer, and attendance at synagogue services.

BIBLICAL TOUCHSTONE

Read 1 Corinthians 15:1-11, where St. Paul tells of how Jesus appeared to men after His Resurrection.

- **How does St. Paul say that he received the gospel?**

- **To whom did Jesus first appear? Then to whom? Who does St. Paul say was last?**

- **Why does St. Paul call himself "least of the apostles"?**

- **What are some things Paul did to cooperate with God's providence?**

SCRIPTURE AND THE SAINTS

Wisdom 9:9
"Now with you is Wisdom, who knows your works and was present when you made the world."

God is the Creator and the "sovereign master of His plan" (*Catechism of the Catholic Church* 306). And yet, as a sign of His goodness, His plan includes making use of His creatures to bring that plan into being. Indeed, as soon as God created humanity, He did something that signaled that we were created free: He gave people a special responsibility that would allow them to cooperate with divine providence. God's plan for creation was good, and He wanted His creation to share in that good. He told Adam and Eve: "Be fertile and multiply; fill the earth and subdue it. Have dominion over the fish of the sea, the birds of the air, and all the living things that crawl on the earth" (Gen. 1:28). Because He created us in His image, we have the dignity of free will. Although sometimes we aren't aware of how or why God is using us for His plan, we are capable of willingly and openly cooperating with Him. We were made to do so.

Luke 1:38
"Mary said, 'Behold, I am the handmaid of the Lord. May it be done to me according to your word.'"

St. Francis de Sales
"Do not look forward to the changes and chances of this life with fear. Rather, look to them with full confidence that, as they arise, God to whom you belong will in his love enable you to profit by them."

FOCUS QUESTION

St. Paul told the Corinthians, "[W]e are God's co-workers; you are God's field, God's building" (1 Cor. 3:9). Watch for ways in which God invites people to work with Him toward the realization of His divine plan for humanity. How can you be watchful as St. Peter and the other Apostles were?

DISCUSSION QUESTIONS

1. What effect do you think Saul's conversion had on the enemies of Christianity?

2. Why do you think Pilate is suspicious of Gabra?

3. Which character do you believe is the most dishonorable? Which character do you believe is the most virtuous? Explain.

4. When Saul goes on to begin his missionary work to bring the gospel to the Gentiles, he assumes his Greek name, Paul. What signs do you see in this episode about the future role Saul (St. Paul) will play in the Church?

ANALYZING THE EPISODE

In Pilate's palace, Joanna tells Tabitha about Jesus' words in Matthew 19:23-24, 30:

"Then Jesus said to his disciples, 'Amen, I say to you, it will be hard for one who is rich to enter the kingdom of heaven. Again, I say to you, it is easier for a camel to pass through the eye of a needle than for one who is rich to enter the kingdom of God.... But many who are first will be last, and the last will be first.'"

- **What did the Apostles learn from this teaching? How can we learn from it about what matters in this world versus the next?**

GO FORTH AND EVANGELIZE

In this episode we see many characters endure suffering: Saul and Joanna are imprisoned; Tabitha is beaten.

This week, make an effort to help those who are suffering.

- Volunteer at a crisis pregnancy center, a shelter for abused women, or an abortion recovery group.

- If you know someone who is going through a struggle that you yourself have gone through, offer him comfort and encouragement.

- If your church has a sister parish in a developing country, organize a special food or clothing drive for members of that church.

CLOSING PRAYER

Pray the prayer of Mary, the *Magnificat*. Mary cooperated with God's divine plan despite first being troubled by the news of the very special role God wanted her to play.

My soul magnifies the Lord
And my spirit rejoices in God my Savior;
Because He has regarded the lowliness of His handmaid;
For behold, henceforth all generations shall call me blessed;
Because He who is mighty has done great things for me,
and holy is His name;
And His mercy is from generation to generation
on those who fear Him.

He has shown might with His arm,
He has scattered the proud in the conceit of their heart.
He has put down the mighty from their thrones,
and has exalted the lowly.
He has filled the hungry with good things,
and the rich He has sent away empty.
He has given help to Israel, his servant, mindful of His mercy
Even as he spoke to our fathers, to Abraham and to his posterity forever.

EPISODE 11
"I Say to You, Arise!"

39
Saul Begins Journey
Back to Tarsus

33
Christ Rises
from the
Dead

46
St. Paul's First
Missionary
Journey

64
Persecution
of Christians
Begins

71-80
Coliseu
Built

IN THIS EPISODE

- St. James negotiates peace between the Christians and the Temple.

- An angel of the Lord speaks to St. Philip and tells him to take the desert road to Gaza.

- Joanna is executed by the Romans.

- Gabra encounters St. Philip on his way home and is converted to Christianity.

- The statue of Caligula arrives in Jerusalem.

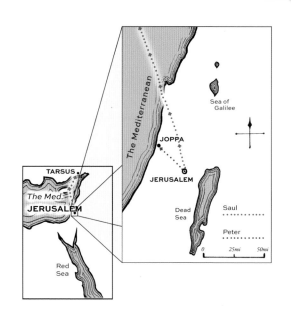

KEY CHARACTERS

"Claudia" is the wife of Pontius Pilate. In this episode, she tries in vain to free Joanna from her Roman captors. *Read more on Claudia in the "Terms to Know" on page 28.*

Cornelius is a Roman centurion. Pilate orders him to carry out Joanna's execution.

Joanna is a disciple of Christ and the wife of Herod Antipas's house manager, Chuza. She is one of the women who first witnessed the Resurrection (Luke 24:10). Her execution by Pilate is fictionalized for the series.

James the Just was, according to tradition, the first bishop of Jerusalem. In this episode, his character negotiates peace between the Christians and the Temple.

Pontius Pilate is the prefect of the Roman province of Judea. The historical Pilate was removed from office in A.D. 36, several years before Caligula gave the order for his statue to be placed in the Temple.

THE CATHOLIC TAKEAWAY

The sacraments are effective signs of grace, instituted by Christ and entrusted by Him to the Church. All the sacraments do what they say they do and are not just symbols.

Apostolic Succession

BY MIKE AQUILINA

Legitimate succession was always a matter of concern in biblical religion. The book of Genesis is careful to give the lineage of the patriarchs, from the first man, Adam, to Noah (Gen. 5). The book of Exodus takes similar care as it sets down the priestly generations (Exod. 6). The Chronicles make clear that the monarchy was legitimately passed from father to son (1 Chron. 3). Indeed, the Old Testament histories assure us that "all Israel was enrolled by genealogies" (1 Chron. 9:1).

And the concern for lineage did not pass away in the New Testament. To establish Jesus' credentials as Messiah, the Gospels detailed His lineage through generations, going back to Abraham (Mt. 1) and even through Adam to God (Luke 3).

In the Old Testament, succession took place in the natural order, through genetic transmission. In the apostolic age, we see a new principle at work. St. Paul was a man who made a firm commitment to live a celibate life (see 1 Cor. 7:1, 7-8), yet he could pass along the grace he had received — by means of the same act by which he himself received the grace: the laying on of hands (Acts 13:2-3).

St. Paul discussed the act in his later letters to Timothy, whom he had ordained (1 Tim. 4:14; 5:22; 2 Tim. 1:6). From Paul we learn that ordination is a "gift of God," although it is conferred by one man upon another. We know that it is a supernatural event consummated by the prayers of those who are authorized to give such "prophetic utterance." We know that the gift is given through "elders" in the Faith to those of a new generation in ministry — who will in turn give it to another generation. As the Father sent the Son, so the Son sent the Apostles — and so the Apostles sent their disciples to serve as bishops.

As time passed and the Faith spread to new lands, the Church valued apostolic succession all the more. It was a safeguard against heresy. The Church could point to a succession that was public and sacramental, whose authenticity could be easily verified. One of Paul's Roman disciples, a man named Clement, spoke of the matter:

> Apostolic succession was a safeguard against heresy. The Church could point to a succession that was public and sacramental, whose authenticity could be easily verified.

The Apostles received the Gospel for us from the Lord Jesus Christ; Jesus Christ was sent forth from God. So Christ is from God, and the Apostles are from Christ. Both therefore came of the will of God in the appointed order. Having received their orders . . . they went forth with the good news that the kingdom of God was to come. So preaching everywhere, in country and town, they appointed their first-fruits, when they had proved them by the Spirit, to be bishops and deacons to those who should believe. . . .

Our Apostles knew through our Lord Jesus Christ that there would be contention over the office of bishop. That is why, having received complete foreknowledge, they appointed the aforesaid persons, and afterward they gave the offices a permanent character, that if these should fall asleep, other approved men should succeed to their ministry (Saint Clement of Rome, *To the Corinthians* 42:1-4; 44:1-2).

And so they still succeed today, to the offices established by the Apostles.

To learn more about the lives and sacrifices of those first Christians given the task of spreading the gospel, read *Ministers and Martyrs: The Ultimate Catholic Guide to the Apostolic Age.*

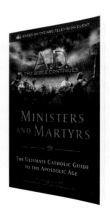

TERMS TO KNOW

- **"Like a lamb he was led to the slaughter":** On his way back from Jerusalem, the eunuch was reading the following prophecy from Isaiah, which was fulfilled by Christ:

  "Though harshly treated, he
  	submitted and did not open his
  	mouth;
  Like a lamb led to slaughter
  	or a sheep silent before shearers,
  	he did not open his mouth.
  Seized and condemned, he was
  	taken away.

  Who would have thought any more of his destiny?" (Isa. 53:7-8).

- **Sacrament:** An outward sign to give grace. The sacraments were instituted by Christ and entrusted by Him to the Church. There are seven sacraments: Baptism, Confirmation, Eucharist, Matrimony, Holy Orders, Reconciliation, and Anointing of the Sick.

- **Synagogue:** A Jewish house of prayer and worship. In Jesus' time, there were more than 480 synagogues in Jerusalem.

BIBLICAL TOUCHSTONE

Read Acts 8:26-40. Think about the trust St. Philip had in the Lord as he embarked on new and hazardous journeys in the name of Jesus. Then reflect on the many times the Lord has told us not to be afraid but to trust in His providence. For example:

- **Acts 10:34-35**
  "Then Peter proceeded to speak and said, 'In truth, I see that God shows no partiality. Rather, in every nation whoever fears him and acts uprightly is acceptable to him.'"

SCRIPTURE AND THE SAINTS

James 5:14-15

"Is anyone among you sick? He should summon the presbyters of the church, and they should pray over him and anoint [him] with oil in the name of the Lord, and the prayer of faith will save the sick person, and the Lord will raise him up. If he has committed any sins, he will be forgiven."

Jesus showed compassion to those who were sick and suffering by healing them and, in some cases, by bringing back to life those who had succumbed to sickness. And He heals not only our bodies, but our souls. For these reasons, we sometimes call Jesus "Christ the Physician." In the sacraments He entrusted to the Church, He continues to touch and heal us.

An effect of Anointing of the Sick is that our suffering is united to Jesus' suffering on the Cross. Anything that Jesus did was made new and made holy. Because He suffered so terribly, we can unite our suffering with His and, in this way, participate in the redemptive quality of suffering for ourselves and for others. The Church asks us all to offer up our suffering, as Jesus did, for the sake of others.

 Did you know?

Pope Francis pointed out that Jesus never healed people only to then leave them alone. He said, "These gestures of Jesus teach us that every healing, every (act of) pardon, always helps us return to our People, which is the Church."

 St. Maximilian Kolbe

"Jesus . . . said to them . . . , 'Those who are well do not need a physician, but the sick do. I did not come to call the righteous but sinners.'"

FOCUS QUESTION

Jesus commanded the Apostles, "Cure the sick, raise the dead, cleanse lepers, drive out demons. Without cost you have received; without cost you are to give" (Mt. 10:8). What signs of their obedience to this command do you see in this episode? How does your own priest carry out this responsibility?

DISCUSSION QUESTIONS

1. In this episode, Peter leaves Jerusalem because of a fictionalized conflict with James the Just. According to Acts chapter 9, why does he leave?

2. The Bible tells of how the disciple Tabitha fell sick and died (Acts 9:36). Under what circumstances does she die in this episode? How does the episode plot differ from Scripture?

3. St. Philip hadn't planned to go to Gaza. What if he had refused the angel's directions, trusting in his own plans instead? Why do you think he didn't?

4. What does Gabra's question about understanding the Scriptures teach us about the authority of our apostolic Church?

5. The conversion of the Ethiopian eunuch involved miracles. An angel of the Lord told St. Philip to take the desert road to Gaza, and then Philip was mysteriously swept away by the Holy Spirit after the eunuch was baptized. We may not witness such dramatic signs and wonders in our daily lives. Yet God is just as present to us. Have you ever tried to pay special attention to the people the Lord puts in your path? Are they seeking something? Can you share with them the truth and love of the gospel message? What might they be able to teach you to help you grow closer to Christ?

ANALYZING THE EPISODE

Read how Peter restores Tabitha to life in Acts 9:36-43.

PETER: Tabitha, rise up.

- **Compare Peter's healing with Jesus' miracle recounted in Mark 5:41: "He took the child by the hand and said to her, 'Talitha koum,' which means, 'Little girl, I say to you, arise!'"**

- **How is Peter's miraculous healing of Tabitha like Jesus' miraculous healings? How is it different?**

GO FORTH AND EVANGELIZE

We may not be able to heal the sick in the same miraculous way Christ did, but we can give of ourselves to help our friends and family and care for people who are sick. Visiting the sick is one of the Corporal Works of Mercy, which are actions Catholics take to bring God's mercy and compassion to others.

The extraordinary stories often associated with Anointing of the Sick provide a wonderful witness to the heroic nature of the priesthood. Interview your parish priest about his own experiences in administering the sacrament of Anointing of the Sick. You might consider asking:

- What is special about Anointing of the Sick among the sacraments?

- How does the sacrament fit into the big scheme of our life on earth and God's will that we return to Him in heaven?

- Can you tell an extraordinary story associated with your administering of Anointing of the Sick?

- Do you think you have witnessed any miracles associated with the sacrament?

CLOSING PRAYER

Bishop Fulton Sheen wrote, "Pain, agony, disappointments, injustices — all these can be poured into a heavenly treasury from which the anemic, sinful, confused, ignorant souls may draw unto the healing of their wings." This week, offer up your own suffering and trials for the sake of others.

Dear Lord,
Help me to remember in these troubled times
The cross you carried for my sake,
So that I may better carry mine
And to help others do the same,

As I offer up [*tell God the problem you are enduring*] to you
For the conversion of sinners,
For the forgiveness of sins,
In reparation for sins,
And for the salvation of souls. Amen.

EPISODE 12

"Whoever Listens to You Listens to Me."

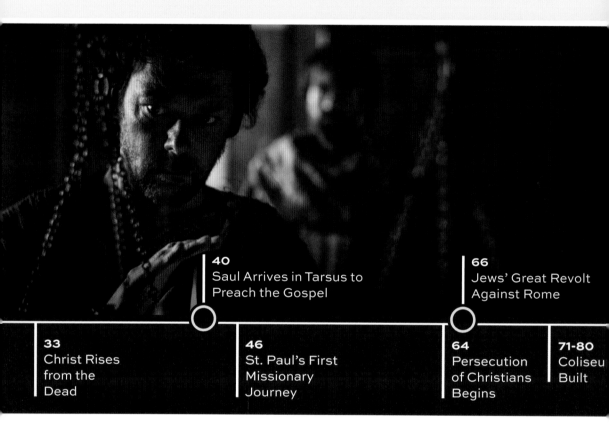

40
Saul Arrives in Tarsus to Preach the Gospel

66
Jews' Great Revolt Against Rome

33
Christ Rises from the Dead

46
St. Paul's First Missionary Journey

64
Persecution of Christians Begins

71-80
Coliseu Built

IN THIS EPISODE

- Peter preaches the Kerygma to Cornelius and his family.

- A centurion becomes the first Roman to be baptized a Christian.

- Caiaphas refuses to help install the statue of Caligula in the Temple and promises peaceful resistance.

- War is coming to Jerusalem.

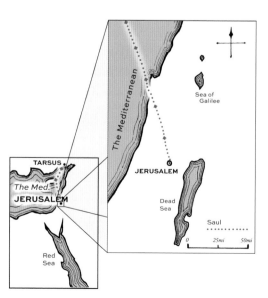

KEY CHARACTERS

 Caiaphas is the Jewish high priest. He refuses to help install the statue of Caligula in the Temple and promises peaceful resistance.

 Cornelius is a Roman centurion. He receives a vision to seek out Peter, who baptizes him a Christian. Still a Roman soldier, he is given the job of killing all who object to the installation of Caligula's statue in the Temple. *For more information on the biblical Cornelius, see "Terms to Know" on page 106.*

 "Eva" is the fiancée of "Boaz"; both are fictionalized for the series. In this episode Eva kills Leah for sowing so much discord among the Jewish people.

 "Leah" is the wife of Caiaphas. She schemes to replace her husband with a new high priest.

 St. Peter is head of the Apostles. He baptizes the first Roman convert to Christianity, a centurion named Cornelius.

 Pontius Pilate was the prefect of the Roman province of Judea. The historical Pilate was removed from office in A.D. 36, several years before Caligula gave the order for his statue to be placed in the Temple.

THE CATHOLIC TAKEAWAY

Scripture alone is not enough to tell us everything we need to know about salvation in Jesus Christ. Sacred Scripture cannot be separated from Sacred Tradition.

The Destruction of Jerusalem

BY MIKE AQUILINA

Disaster was looming for Jerusalem. Radical groups were growing, and the occupying powers grew increasingly uneasy. As far back as A.D. 39, the Roman emperor Caligula had uncovered a plot to overthrow Roman rule. Furious, he responded by reorganizing the territory and rewarding the leaders most loyal to Rome. When Jews in Egypt rioted against local authorities, Caligula reacted with the most outrageously offensive order imaginable. He commanded that a statue of himself be raised in the Jerusalem Temple. His aides knew that this would be an act of war, but Caligula — who was known for his violent temper and whom many suspected to be insane — would not back down. But bureaucrats dragged their feet, and the project was delayed long enough for even Caligula to see its madness. He reversed his order.

But the damage was done. The Jews and the Romans, always suspicious of one another, were now further estranged. Other incidents followed — attacks on Roman citizens became more frequent. Gentiles, for their part, began to taunt their Jewish neighbors. In the year 66, some Greeks sacrificed birds in front of a synagogue, while the Romans looked on and did nothing. Outraged, the Temple priests put a stop to all sacrifices offered for the good of Caesar. The Roman procurator reacted by sending troops to the Temple to make a huge withdrawal of gold from the treasury — a gift for the emperor.

Now came war. From the Roman perspective, it seemed to come from many directions. There were countless cells of disaffected men — and sects of warriors inspired by prophecy. All closed in on the imperial troops and government. So began the bloodshed that came to be known as the first Roman-Jewish War.

The war raged from A.D. 66 to 73, but its climax was a seven-month siege of Jerusalem in the year 70. The Romans sealed off all the city's supply routes and stopped up its water supply. By midsum-

> By midsummer that year, the Romans had breached the walls, and at the end of July the city was in flames. On July 29, the Temple — Herod's grand reconstruction, which had only recently been completed — was destroyed.

mer that year, the Romans had breached the walls, and at the end of July the city was in flames. On July 29, the Temple — Herod's grand reconstruction, which had only recently been completed — was destroyed. The Christians had long since left the city, warned by a prophecy given to the Church.

Both Christians and Jews came to see the destruction of Jerusalem as God's judgment on a sinful generation. At that point, however, their interpretations parted ways. For the Jews, sacrifice ceased with the utter destruction and profanation of the Temple. For Christians, however, the age of pure sacrifice was just beginning. They recalled that, at Jesus' death, "the curtain of the temple was torn in two, from top to bottom" (Mt. 27:51). The Temple thus had been decommissioned, made obsolete by Jesus' sacrifice.

Now the Temple was Christ. Now the Temple was His Church. So close was the communion of Christ with His Church.

That was the Gospel of Jesus Christ as it was proclaimed in the apostolic age, by the Church through its ministers and martyrs.

To learn more about the lives and sacrifices of those first Christians given the task of spreading the gospel, read *Ministers and Martyrs: The Ultimate Catholic Guide to the Apostolic Age*.

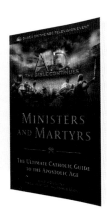

TERMS TO KNOW

- **Centurion:** An officer in the Roman army.

- **Cornelius:** Although the character of "Cornelius" is fictionalized for the series, the first Roman to be converted to Christianity was in fact a centurion named Cornelius. The biblical Cornelius served in a battalion of archers in Caesarea and was not a lieutenant of Pilate.

- **Doxology:** A prayer of praise to God.

- **Gentiles:** People not of the Jewish nation or the Jewish faith.

- **Kerygma:** *Kerygma* is the Greek word κήρυγμα, which is used nine times in the New Testament to mean the preaching or proclamation of the essential gospel message that invites a person to conversion. For examples, see Matthew 12:41; Mark 16:20; Luke 11:32; Romans 16:25; 1 Corinthians 1:21, 2:4, 15:14; 2 Timothy 4:17; and Titus 1:3.

- **Magisterium of the Church:** The teaching office of the Church, made up of the pope and the bishops in communion with him. Going back to St. Peter, bishop of Rome, the Magisterium has had the sole authority to interpret the Word of God. As the servant of the Word of God, the Magisterium teaches only what has been handed on to it by Jesus Christ.

BIBLICAL TOUCHSTONE

The baptism of Cornelius is recounted in Acts chapter 10. Read St. Peter's speech to Cornelius's household in Acts 10:34-43.

- **This speech is a good example of the way early Christians preached to Gentiles. What are some if its qualities?**

- **What clues do you see in this passage about the authority entrusted by Jesus to the Apostles?**

- **The Old Covenant was between God and His Chosen People of Israel. Why is it so significant that Jesus told the Apostles to bring His message to the Gentiles? What does this mean about the New Covenant?**

SCRIPTURE AND THE SAINTS

Luke 10:16
"Whoever listens to you listens to me. Whoever rejects you rejects me. And whoever rejects me rejects the one who sent me."

The entire Word of God is found in Sacred Scripture and Sacred Tradition. These heavenly gifts are tied together and flow from the same divine source: our Triune God. The Holy Spirit did not simply inspire the authors of the sacred books and then back off. Rather, God, who became man to be with us, remains with us in our bishops and priests and in the sacred traditions He imparted to the first bishops with whom He walked on Earth. "Sacred Scripture and Sacred Tradition make present and fruitful in the Church the mystery of Christ, who promised to remain with his own 'always, to the close of the age'" (*Catechism of the Catholic Church* 80).

Sacred Tradition is not something that gets in the way of our understanding of who God is and what He is calling us to do. Rather, Sacred Tradition is essential for understanding the truths of our Faith, which goes back to the time of the Apostles. "Scripture is to be proclaimed, heard, read, received and experienced as the word of God, in the stream of the apostolic Tradition from which it is inseparable" (*Verbum Domini* 7). Each relies on the other, and both are necessary.

 Did you know?
The idea that Scripture alone is the highest source of Christian doctrine and practice does not appear in the Bible.

 St. Bernard of Clairvaux
"The Word is 'not a written and mute word, but the Word which is incarnate and living.'"

 1 Corinthians 11:1-2
"Be imitators of me, as I am of Christ. I praise you because you remember me in everything and hold fast to the traditions, just as I handed them on to you."

1 Thessalonians 2:13

"[I]n receiving the word of God from hearing us, you received not a human word but, as it truly is, the word of God, which is now at work in you who believe."

2 Thessalonians 2:15

"Therefore, brothers, stand firm and hold fast to the traditions that you were taught, either by an oral statement or by a letter of ours."

2 Timothy 2:2

"And what you heard from me through many witnesses entrust to faithful people who will have the ability to teach others as well."

FOCUS QUESTION

Jesus Christ gave us a model of the perfect life. How did He share the truth with others? Why do you think He didn't write anything down Himself? Wouldn't this have made it easier for us all to understand how to get to heaven?

DISCUSSION QUESTIONS

1. In Jesus' time, the Gentiles were considered unclean by Jews. What signs do we see in this episode that this law has been changed by Jesus?

2. Why is it important that the Apostles brought Jesus' message to the Gentiles?

3. In the biblical account of the conversion of Cornelius, Cornelius initially bows before St. Peter, paying him homage. Peter, however, raised him up, saying, "Get up. I myself am also a human being" (Acts 10:26). Why does he say this? Who is the only proper object of our adoration?

4. Why do you think Jesus revealed Himself only to simple fishermen, a tax collector, and other ordinary people?

5. What are you feeling as the series draws to a close? Was this a good end point to the story? What do you think will happen next? How can you find out?

ANALYZING THE EPISODE

St. Peter baptizes the first Gentile, a centurion named Cornelius.

PETER: This man God raised [on] the third day and granted that he be visible, not to all the people, but to us, the witnesses chosen by God in advance, who ate and drank with him after he rose from the dead. He commissioned us to preach to the people and testify that he is the one appointed by God as judge of the living and the dead (Acts 10:40-42).

What are some reasons St. Peter says these things to Cornelius?

GO FORTH AND EVANGELIZE

Our Catholic Faith has been handed down to us through apostolic succession from the time of Christ. This week, as the series comes to an end, make a special effort to memorize the Apostles' Creed, if you haven't already, and to share this clear and concise statement of our Faith with family and friends:

I believe in God,
the Father almighty,
Creator of heaven and earth,
and in Jesus Christ, his only Son,
our Lord,
who was conceived by the Holy Spirit,
born of the Virgin Mary,
suffered under Pontius Pilate,
was crucified, died, and was buried;
he descended into hell;
on the third day he rose again from
the dead;

he ascended into heaven,
and is seated at the right hand of God,
the Father almighty;
from there he will come to judge the
living and the dead.
I believe in the Holy Spirit,
the holy catholic Church,
the communion of saints,
the forgiveness of sins,
the resurrection of the body,
and life everlasting.
AMEN.

CLOSING PRAYER

The beloved disciple closed his Gospel by reflecting on the many things that Jesus did. There were so many, he said, that it would be impossible to write them all down! "There are also many other things that Jesus did, but if these were to be described individually, I do not think the whole world would contain the books that would be written" (John 21:25). This week, reflect on the things you have learned about our Faith throughout the series, and all the infinite wonders of our Lord, and the gifts He has given us to help us be close to Him in Sacred Scripture and Sacred Tradition.

Pray a doxology:

Glory be to the Father, and to the Son, and to the Holy Spirit. As it was in the beginning, is now and ever shall be, world without end. AMEN.

You may also wish to say it in Latin, the language of ancient Rome and the official language of the Church:

Gloria Patri, et Filio, et Spiritui Sancto.
Sicut erat in principio,
et nunc,
et semper,
et in saecula saeculorum. AMEN.

NOTES

NOTES

NOTES

NOTES